DIGITAL SIGNATURE ALGORITHM: LEARN BY EXAMPLES WITH PYTHON AND TKINTER

VIVIAN SIAHAAN
RISMON HASIHOLAN SIANIPAR

Copyright © 2024 BALIGE Publishing

All rights reserved. No part of this book may be reproduced, stored in a retrieval system, or transmitted in any form or by any means, without the prior written permission of the publisher, except in the case of brief quotations embedded in critical articles or reviews. Every effort has been made in the preparation of this book to ensure the accuracy of the information presented. However, the information contained in this book is sold without warranty, either express or implied. Neither the authors, nor BALIGE Publishing or its dealers and distributors, will be held liable for any damages caused or alleged to have been caused directly or indirectly by this book. BALIGE Publishing has endeavored to provide trademark information about all of the companies and products mentioned in this book by the appropriate use of capitals. However, BALIGE Publishing cannot guarantee the accuracy of this information.

Published: SEPTEMBER 2024
Production reference: 0700924
Published by BALIGE Publishing Ltd.
BALIGE, North Sumatera

ABOUT THE AUTHOR

Vivian Siahaan is a highly motivated individual with a passion for continuous learning and exploring new areas. Born and raised in Hinalang Bagasan, Balige, situated on the picturesque banks of Lake Toba, she completed her high school education at SMAN 1 Balige. Vivian's journey into the world of programming began with a deep dive into various languages such as Java, Android, JavaScript, CSS, C++, Python, R, Visual Basic, Visual C#, MATLAB, Mathematica, PHP, JSP, MySQL, SQL Server, Oracle, Access, and more. Starting from scratch, Vivian diligently studied programming, focusing on mastering the fundamental syntax and logic. She honed her skills by creating practical GUI applications, gradually building her expertise. One particular area of interest for Vivian is animation and game development, where she aspires to make significant contributions. Alongside her programming and mathematical pursuits, she also finds joy in indulging in novels, nurturing her love for literature. Vivian Siahaan's passion for programming and her extensive knowledge are reflected in the numerous ebooks she has authored. Her works, published by Sparta Publisher, cover a wide range of topics, including "Data Structure with Java," "Java Programming: Cookbook," "C++ Programming: Cookbook," "C Programming For High Schools/Vocational Schools and Students," "Java Programming for SMA/SMK," "Java Tutorial: GUI, Graphics and Animation," "Visual Basic Programming: From A to Z," "Java Programming for Animation and Games," "C# Programming for SMA/SMK and Students," "MATLAB For Students and Researchers," "Graphics in JavaScript: Quick Learning Series," "JavaScript Image Processing Methods: From A to Z," "Java GUI Case Study: AWT & Swing," "Basic CSS and JavaScript," "PHP/MySQL Programming: Cookbook," "Visual Basic: Cookbook," "C++ Programming for High Schools/Vocational Schools and Students," "Concepts and Practices of C++," "PHP/MySQL For Students," "C# Programming: From A to Z," "Visual Basic for SMA/SMK and Students," and "C# .NET and SQL Server for High School/Vocational School and Students." Furthermore, at the ANDI Yogyakarta publisher, Vivian Siahaan has contributed to several notable books, including "Python Programming Theory and Practice," "Python GUI Programming," "Python GUI and Database," "Build From Zero School Database Management System In Python/MySQL," "Database Management System in Python/MySQL," "Python/MySQL For Management Systems of Criminal Track Record Database," "Java/MySQL For Management Systems of Criminal Track Records Database," "Database and Cryptography Using Java/MySQL," and "Build From Zero School Database Management System With Java/MySQL." Vivian's diverse range of expertise in programming languages, combined with her passion for exploring new horizons, makes her a dynamic and versatile individual in the field of technology. Her dedication to learning, coupled with her strong analytical and problem-solving skills, positions her as a valuable asset in any programming endeavor. Vivian Siahaan's contributions to the world of programming and literature continue to inspire and empower aspiring programmers and readers alike.

Rismon Hasiholan Sianipar, born in Pematang Siantar in 1994, is a distinguished researcher and expert in the field of electrical engineering. After completing his education at SMAN 3 Pematang Siantar, Rismon ventured to the city of Jogjakarta to pursue his academic journey. He obtained his Bachelor of Engineering (S.T) and Master of Engineering (M.T) degrees in Electrical Engineering from Gadjah Mada University in 1998 and 2001, respectively, under the guidance of esteemed professors, Dr. Adhi Soesanto and Dr. Thomas Sri Widodo. During his studies, Rismon focused on researching non-stationary signals and their energy analysis using time-frequency maps. He explored the dynamic nature of signal energy distribution on time-frequency maps and developed innovative techniques using discrete wavelet transformations to design non-linear filters for data pattern analysis. His research showcased the application of these techniques in various fields. In recognition of his academic prowess, Rismon was awarded the prestigious Monbukagakusho scholarship by the Japanese Government in 2003. He went on to pursue his Master of Engineering (M.Eng) and Doctor of Engineering (Dr.Eng) degrees at Yamaguchi University, supervised by Prof. Dr. Hidetoshi Miike. Rismon's master's and doctoral theses revolved around combining the SR-FHN (Stochastic Resonance Fitzhugh-Nagumo) filter strength with the cryptosystem ECC (elliptic curve cryptography) 4096-bit. This innovative approach effectively suppressed noise in digital images and videos while ensuring their authenticity. Rismon's research findings have been published in renowned international scientific journals, and his patents have been officially registered in Japan. Notably, one of his patents, with registration number 2008-009549, gained recognition. He actively collaborates with several universities and research institutions in Japan, specializing in cryptography, cryptanalysis, and digital forensics, particularly in the areas of audio, image, and video analysis. With a passion for knowledge sharing, Rismon has authored numerous national and international scientific articles and authored several national books. He has also actively participated in workshops related to cryptography, cryptanalysis, digital watermarking, and digital forensics. During these workshops, Rismon has assisted Prof. Hidetoshi Miike in developing applications related to digital image and video processing, steganography, cryptography, watermarking, and more, which serve as valuable training materials. Rismon's field of interest encompasses multimedia security, signal processing, digital image and video analysis, cryptography, digital communication, digital forensics, and data compression. He continues to advance his research by developing applications using programming languages such as Python, MATLAB, C++, C, VB.NET, C#.NET, R, and Java. These applications serve both research and commercial purposes, further contributing to the advancement of signal and image analysis. Rismon Hasiholan Sianipar is a dedicated researcher and expert in the field of electrical engineering, particularly in the areas of signal processing, cryptography, and digital forensics. His academic achievements, patented inventions, and extensive publications demonstrate his commitment to advancing knowledge in these fields. Rismon's contributions to academia and his collaborations with prestigious institutions in Japan have solidified his position as a respected figure in the scientific community. Through his ongoing research and development of innovative applications, Rismon continues to make significant contributions to the field of electrical engineering.

ABOUT THE BOOK

Project 1 demonstrates generating a DSA (Digital Signature Algorithm) key pair using the cryptography library, where a 2048-bit private key is created and a corresponding public key is derived. The private key is essential for securely signing digital messages, and the public key allows others to verify these signatures. Both keys are serialized into PEM format, making them suitable for storage or transmission. The private key is serialized without encryption (though encryption is optional), while the public key is also serialized for easy sharing and use in cryptographic operations.

Project 2 is a DSA (Digital Signature Algorithm) Key Generator application built with Python's tkinter for the GUI and the cryptography library for key generation. It provides an intuitive interface to generate, view, and save 2048-bit DSA key pairs, essential for secure digital signatures. The GUI features two tabs: "Generate Keys" for creating and serializing keys into PEM format, and "View Keys" for displaying them. Users can save the keys as .pem files with ease, supported by robust error handling and success notifications, making the application accessible and practical for secure communication needs.

Project 3 demonstrates the process of signing and verifying a message using the Digital Signature Algorithm (DSA) in Python, while ensuring the signature is UTF-8 safe by encoding it in Base64. It begins by generating a DSA private and public key pair with a key size of 2048 bits. A message (in bytes) is then created, which is the data to be signed. The private key is used to generate a digital signature for the message using the SHA-256 hashing algorithm, ensuring the integrity and authenticity of the message. The generated signature, which is binary data, is encoded into Base64 format to make it text-safe and suitable for UTF-8 encoding.

To verify the signature, the Base64-encoded signature is first decoded back into its original binary form. The public key is then used to verify the authenticity of the signature by comparing it to the message. If the verification is successful, the message "Signature is valid." is printed; otherwise, an InvalidSignature exception is raised, and the message "Signature is invalid." is displayed. This approach ensures that the digital signature can be safely transmitted or stored as text without data corruption, while still preserving its security properties.

Project 4 is a Tkinter-based GUI application for Digital Signature Algorithm (DSA) operations, offering an intuitive interface for generating DSA keys, signing messages, and verifying signatures. It has two main tabs: one for generating and displaying DSA key pairs in PEM format, and another for signing and verifying messages. Users can input a message, sign it with the private key, and view the Base64-encoded signature, or verify a signature against the original message using the public key. The application handles errors gracefully, providing feedback on operations, making it a practical tool for cryptographic tasks.

Project 5 and 6 provides a complete implementation for generating, signing, and verifying files using the Digital Signature Algorithm (DSA). It includes functions for creating DSA key pairs, signing file contents, and verifying signatures. The generate_and_save_keys() function generates a private and public key, serializes them to PEM format, and saves them to files. The sign_file() function uses the private key to sign the SHA-256 hash of a file's content, saving the signature in Base64 format. The verify_file_signature() function then verifies this signature using the public key, ensuring the file's authenticity and integrity.

The project is designed as a user-friendly Tkinter-based GUI application, with three main functionalities: key generation, file signing, and signature verification. Users can generate DSA key pairs in the "Generate Keys" tab, sign files in the "Sign File" tab, and verify signatures in the "Verify Signature" tab. By providing an intuitive interface, this application enables users to efficiently manage cryptographic operations, ensuring data security and authenticity without needing to understand low-level cryptographic details.

Project 7 and 8 focuses on creating and securing synthetic financial datasets to ensure data integrity. It combines data generation, digital signing, and signature verification to authenticate and protect financial records. The primary goals are to generate realistic financial data, secure it with digital signatures, and verify these signatures to detect tampering or corruption.

The project involves generating a synthetic dataset with multiple columns such as transaction IDs, account numbers, amounts, currencies, timestamps, and transaction types. DSA keys are then generated for signing and verification, with the private key used for signing each entry in the dataset. These signatures are saved separately, allowing verification using the public key. This process ensures that any unauthorized changes to the data are detected, demonstrating a secure approach to data handling in financial applications.

Project 9 and 10 combines the Digital Signature Algorithm (DSA) with Least Significant Bit (LSB) steganography to securely hide a signed message within an image. First, DSA keys are generated and used to sign a message, ensuring its authenticity and integrity. The signed message is then embedded into an image using LSB steganography, where the least significant bits of the image pixels' red channel are altered to include the binary representation of the message and its signature.

To extract and verify the hidden data, the code retrieves the embedded bits from the image and reconstructs the original message. It then uses the public DSA key to verify the signature, confirming the message's authenticity. This integration of cryptographic signing with steganography provides a secure method to conceal and authenticate sensitive information within an image file.

Project 11 and 12 provides a workflow for encrypting and hiding data using RSA and DSA cryptographic algorithms, along with steganography. It begins with generating RSA and DSA keys, then encrypts a message using RSA and signs it with a DSA private key, ensuring confidentiality and authenticity. The encrypted and signed data is embedded into an image using Least Significant Bit (LSB) steganography, altering the pixel values to include the hidden information.

The process continues by extracting the hidden data from the image, verifying its integrity using the DSA signature, and decrypting the message with the RSA private key. This approach demonstrates a secure method of combining encryption, digital signatures, and steganography to protect and authenticate sensitive data, making it a robust solution for secure data transmission.

CONTENT

Project 1: Demonstrating DSA Key Generation	3
Project 2: GUI Tkinter for Demonstrating DSA Key Generation	8
Project 3: Signing and Verifying DSA Signature	15
Project 4: GUI Tkinter for Signing and Verifying DSA Signature	18
Project 5: Signing and Verifying File	30
Project 6: GUI Tkinter for Signing and Verifying File	40
Project 7: Managing Data Integrity and Security on Synthetic Financial Dataset	63
Project 8: GUI Tkinter for Managing Data Integrity and Security on Synthetic Financial Dataset	72
Project 9: Hiding Confidential Message with DSA and LSB Steganography	92
Project 10: GUI Tkinter for Hiding Confidential Message with DSA and LSB Steganography	114
Project 11: Hiding Confidential Message with RSA and DSA Cryptographics Algorithm and LSB Steganography	132
Project 12: GUI Tkinter for Hiding Confidential Message with RSA and DSA Cryptographics Algorithm and LSB Steganography	143
BIBLIOGRAPHY	151

DIGITAL SIGNATURE ALGORITHM (DSA)

INTRODUCTION

The Digital Signature Algorithm (DSA) is a cryptographic algorithm used for generating digital signatures, providing both authentication and data integrity. It was proposed by the National Institute of Standards and Technology (NIST) in 1991 and is widely used in digital communication protocols. Here's how it works and its key concepts:

How DSA Works
DSA involves two processes:
1. Signature Generation – Signing the data.
2. Signature Verification – Checking if the signature is valid.

These processes are built on public-key cryptography, where a pair of keys (a private key and a public key) are used.

1. Signature Generation:
- The signer generates a hash of the message using a hash function (such as SHA-256).
- Using the private key, the signer generates a digital signature based on the hash.
- The signature is attached to the original message and sent to the recipient.

2. Signature Verification:
- The recipient receives the message and the signature.
- Using the sender's public key, the recipient verifies the signature by:
  - Hashing the received message.
  - Comparing the result of this hash with the signature using the public key.
- If they match, the signature is valid, confirming that the message has not been altered and is from the expected sender.

Key Concepts
- Private Key: This is used to create the digital signature. It must be kept secret by the sender.
- Public Key: This is used by anyone to verify the authenticity of the signature. It's publicly available.
- Hash Function: DSA uses a cryptographic hash function to compress the message into a fixed-size value (the hash). The hash ensures that the signature process is based on the content of the message, without the need to encrypt the entire message.
- Modular Arithmetic: DSA relies heavily on mathematical operations in finite fields, specifically modular exponentiation, for generating signatures.

Steps in DSA
1. Key Generation:
   - Selects a large prime number p and a prime divisor q of p-1.
   - Chooses a random integer g as the generator of a subgroup of order q in the finite field Z_p.
   - The private key is a random integer x, where $1 < x < q$.
   - The public key is computed as $y = g^x \mod p$.
2. Signature Generation:
   - For each message, a random integer k is selected where $1 < k < q$.
   - Compute $r = (g^k \mod p) \mod q$.
   - Compute $s = (k^{-1} * (H(m) + x * r)) \mod q$, where H(m) is the hash of the message.
   - The signature is the pair (r, s).

3. Signature Verification:
    - Compute w = s^(-1) mod q.
    - Compute u1 = (H(m) * w) mod q and u2 = (r * w) mod q.
    - Compute v = ((g^u1 * y^u2) mod p) mod q.
    - If v == r, the signature is valid.

Security of DSA

The security of DSA relies on the difficulty of the Discrete Logarithm Problem. Breaking DSA would require efficiently solving the discrete logarithm, which is computationally infeasible for sufficiently large key sizes.

Advantages
- Efficiency: DSA is faster in key generation and signature verification than some other algorithms like RSA.
- Widely Used: It is part of many standards, including DSS (Digital Signature Standard) by NIST.

Limitations
- Random Number Vulnerability: If the random number k used in signing is predictable, the private key can be compromised.
- No Encryption: DSA is used only for signatures, not for encrypting messages.

In summary, DSA is a secure and efficient algorithm used to ensure the authenticity and integrity of digital communications by generating and verifying digital signatures.

KEY GENERATION
Project 1: Demonstrating DSA Key Generation

This code demonstrates the generation of a DSA (Digital Signature Algorithm) key pair, where a private key and a corresponding public key are created. It first imports the necessary modules from the cryptography library, including the DSA algorithm and serialization tools. The dsa.generate_private_key() function generates a 2048-bit private key, which is a critical component for signing digital messages securely. From the private key, the public key is derived using the public_key() method. The public key can later be shared with others, allowing them to verify digital signatures created with the private key.

After generating the keys, the private key and public key are serialized into PEM (Privacy Enhanced Mail) format, a common format for storing cryptographic keys. The private key is serialized using the private_bytes() method with the NoEncryption() option, meaning it is stored without password protection (though encryption could be added). Similarly, the public key is serialized using the public_bytes() method. Finally, both the private and public keys are printed in PEM format, making them readable and ready to be saved or transmitted for cryptographic operations like signing or verifying messages.

```python
from cryptography.hazmat.primitives.asymmetric import dsa
from cryptography.hazmat.primitives import serialization

# Generate DSA private key
private_key = dsa.generate_private_key(key_size=2048)

# Generate the corresponding public key
public_key = private_key.public_key()

# Serialize the private key to PEM format (for storage or transmission)
private_pem = private_key.private_bytes(
    encoding=serialization.Encoding.PEM,
    format=serialization.PrivateFormat.TraditionalOpenSSL,
    encryption_algorithm=serialization.NoEncryption()  # No password protection
)

# Serialize the public key to PEM format
public_pem = public_key.public_bytes(
    encoding=serialization.Encoding.PEM,
    format=serialization.PublicFormat.SubjectPublicKeyInfo
)

# Output the generated keys
print("DSA Private Key:")
print(private_pem.decode())

print("DSA Public Key:")
print(public_pem.decode())
```

This code demonstrates how to generate a Digital Signature Algorithm (DSA) key pair in Python using the cryptography library, and how to serialize the keys into the PEM (Privacy Enhanced Mail) format for storage or transmission.

1. Importing Required Modules:

```python
from cryptography.hazmat.primitives.asymmetric import dsa
from cryptography.hazmat.primitives import serialization
```

- The dsa module provides functionalities to create DSA key pairs, which are used for digital signatures.
- The serialization module provides methods for converting keys into byte formats like PEM, which is commonly used for secure key storage or transmission.

2. Generating a DSA Private Key:

```
private_key = dsa.generate_private_key(key_size=2048)
```

- The dsa.generate_private_key() function generates a private key using the DSA algorithm. The key_size=2048 argument specifies the size of the key in bits (2048-bit DSA key), which influences the strength of the cryptography. Larger keys are more secure but slower.
- The private key is stored in the private_key object. This key is confidential and is used to create digital signatures.

3. Deriving the Public Key:

```
public_key = private_key.public_key()
```

- The public_key() method derives the corresponding public key from the private key. In asymmetric cryptography, the private key is kept secret, while the public key can be shared freely.
- The public key is used for verifying signatures created by the corresponding private key. It is stored in the public_key object.

4. Serializing the Private Key to PEM Format:

```
private_pem = private_key.private_bytes(
    encoding=serialization.Encoding.PEM,
    format=serialization.PrivateFormat.TraditionalOpenSSL,
    encryption_algorithm=serialization.NoEncryption()
)
```

- The private_bytes() method serializes the private key into a byte format, making it suitable for storage or transmission. Here, we specify the following parameters:

- encoding=serialization.Encoding.PEM: Specifies that the private key should be encoded in PEM format, which is a Base64-encoded format used to store and transmit cryptographic keys.
- format=serialization.PrivateFormat.TraditionalOpenSSL: This specifies the traditional OpenSSL format for storing private keys.
- encryption_algorithm=serialization.NoEncryption(): This means the private key is stored without any encryption or password protection. In real-world use cases, it is often advisable to encrypt private keys with a passphrase to enhance security.
- The result is stored in private_pem, which contains the private key in PEM format as a byte string.

5. Serializing the Public Key to PEM Format:

```
public_pem = public_key.public_bytes(
    encoding=serialization.Encoding.PEM,
    format=serialization.PublicFormat.SubjectPublicKeyInfo
)
```

- The public_bytes() method serializes the public key to a byte format for storage or transmission, similar to the private key. We specify:
  - encoding=serialization.Encoding.PEM: This encodes the public key in PEM format.
  - format=serialization.PublicFormat.SubjectPublicKeyInfo: This format is used to store public keys in a standard format for sharing and distribution.
- The result is stored in public_pem, which contains the public key in PEM format as a byte string.

6. Printing the PEM-Formatted Keys:

```
print("DSA Private Key:")
print(private_pem.decode())

print("DSA Public Key:")
print(public_pem.decode())
```

- The decode() method is called to convert the byte strings private_pem and public_pem into human-readable strings (i.e., from bytes to UTF-8 encoding).

- The PEM format outputs the key as a string that typically begins with -----BEGIN DSA PRIVATE KEY----- for the private key and -----BEGIN PUBLIC KEY----- for the public key. These headers and footers indicate the type of key and its format.

Output

```
DSA Private Key:
-----BEGIN DSA PRIVATE KEY-----
MIIDVQIBAAKCAQEAmXe7BJaHDrlBzGS9AcUxGVUAG1jKn/ngN7mIly4ugCxs9O9W
dAFKn3vtPgKc2A86qY1xSLBbVBtQJRwqogFK8+IAEq0p1LQtlu/mnupic7Eyvf6T
wPvezm0jt1CagTtNSCOiNMSt0F/MOItFR7U8eUxPaVt+JdUd1JCOtRNWnr0nZP/m
9kITFtkGsELvmVvNrj2e/PxvF3F6k97CIhV4dVRDAPQqw9/zWgDBKBdaXouBor9S
UCC+MatsYi2FMw+epVrr0gnkdlemZy8bPBDGGMvrxbwMqfG7XizO4uP3h2q9bLIT
nwFlDmrgLQDvVQSNx9KmbE6WmX77CuFWgJxm8wIhANBHIC74uJM+Wd8e8UNgNFWR
tvvquSnIkFT6AafGh/JTAoIBAAq3XFCk9Sk9R9H4pCmvHcKHtSwBRy5+JaSEAVFT
PmezQ7+hwMe0EOEk2gTJdrKGJqzyBVnKrxCcrQ0Cqhj+Ycx5yr+iMtXF/HC2OvXS
MA7CrX14TkFnZIIs9s1+MloSoP0Y9Be6dFXEybzhQFjO9EHy+krAYrYNJtuLbSP2
ZFdZt3+TsnrJywhXH4OBGJ/IOol27KrP9mKGTagVZqV4b9QMe3ng6pwTvlfJDazG
n4gI4+DUcvgH+MIs8eNMcLAv6xGuyNCk0iRm/dSi8E8R1oI38Hjf4qQ37JPUrdXj
dbvVjpI03l3lgJFezp8cGh5gRfoyDEgAYdICW4WTgaleCMMCggEAKEAv7gmqR8XC
VJ0rx6CBaKBVMQbXo/LwtFcCqtgmdQ3S0wJeL4ci5m3UcsLSB2lbcDRmsNhYSyL/
U0R2gZ6VG0JjOCnrS6HyXD/nWw4VQ/5FuQMCdDJW+b4wHtq3koESWmKoxx8fWX8N
aJOH/9xnN5K0ZS7ibKkLMGS5WwqJrguVSrVBvSajcaJalJkMn/7N2wdNJHlGJoK2
GAABSa7D4lNIIpZz8E44R4fsKVAkPrRV2ASGVdEmPpv8sM1ZAywp2kpziW5UxoEI
RKRtvl+4Wf26xa0GVVzs/jkE8xmHaZ0eZPLKLqqSeabxaADbnEP2wuU70TXDMD5L
53pAvRkn5AIgF5J6bGqtyaYLliKRt3BFdT3e/pSKhiLKs75lvPAKzrM=
-----END DSA PRIVATE KEY-----

DSA Public Key:
-----BEGIN PUBLIC KEY-----
MIIDRjCCAjkGByqGSM44BAEwggIsAoIBAQCZd7sElocOuUHMZL0BxTEZVQAbWMqf
+eA3uYiXLi6ALGz071Z0AUqfe+0+ApzYDzqpjXFIsFtUG1AlHCqiAUrz4gASrSnU
tC2W7+ae6mJzsTK9/pPA+97ObSO3UJqBO01II6I0xK3QX8w4i0VHtTx5TE9pW34l
1R3UkI61E1aevSdk/+b2QhMW2QawQu+ZW82uPZ78/G8XcXqT3sIiFXh1VEMA9CrD
3/NaAMEoF1pei4Giv1JQIL4xq2xiLYUzD56lWuvSCeR2V6ZnLxs8EMYYy+vFvAyp
8bteLM7i4/eHar1sshOfAXUOauAtAO9VBI3H0qZsTpaZfvsK4VaAnGbzAiEA0Ecg
Lvi4kz5Z3x7xQ2A0VZG2++q5KciQVPoBp8aH8lMCggEACrdcUKT1KT1H0fikKa8d
woelLAFHLn4lpIQBUVM+Z7NDv6HAx7QQ4STaBMl2soYmrPIFWcqvEJytDQKqGP5h
zHnKv6Iy1cX8cLY69dIwDsKtfXhOQWdkgiz2zX4yWhKg/RjOF7p0VcTJvOFAWM70
QfL6SsBitg0m24ttI/ZkV1m3f50yesnLCFcfg4EYn8g6iXbsqs/2YoZNqBVmpXhv
1Ax7eeDqnBO+V8kNrMafiAjj4NRy+Af4wizx40xwsC/rEa7I0KTSJGb91KLwTxHW
gjfweN/ipDfsk9St1eN1u9WOkjTeXeWAkV7OnxwaHmBF+jIMSABh0gJbhZOBqV4I
wwOCAQUAAoIBAChAL+4JqkfFwlSdK8eggWigVTEG16Py8lRXAqrYJnUN0tMCXi+H
IuZt1HLC0gdpW3A0ZrDYWEsi/1NEdoGelRtCYzgp60uh8lw/51sOFUP+RbkDAnQy
Vvm+MB7at5KBElpiqMcfH1l/DWiTh//cZzeStGUu4mypCzBkuVsKia4LlUq1Qb0m
o3GiWpSZDJ/+zdsHTSR5RiaCthgAAUmuw+JTSCKWc/BOOEeH7ClQJD60VdgEhlXR
Jj6b/LDNWQMsKdpKc4luVMaBCESkbb5fuFn9usWtBlVc7P45BPMZh2mdHmTyyi6q
knmm8WgA25xD9sLlO9E1wzA+S+d6QL0ZJ+Q=
-----END PUBLIC KEY-----
```

Project 2: GUI Tkinter for Demonstrating DSA Key Generation

This project is a comprehensive DSA (Digital Signature Algorithm) Key Generator application built using Python's tkinter library for the graphical user interface (GUI) and the cryptography library for cryptographic operations. The primary goal of the application is to provide users with an intuitive and user-friendly tool to generate, view, and save DSA key pairs, which are essential for digital signatures and ensuring secure communication. By leveraging tkinter, the application offers a visually organized interface with tabs, buttons, and text areas, making the process of key generation accessible even to those with limited technical expertise. The use of cryptography ensures that the keys generated adhere to robust security standards, utilizing a 2048-bit key size to provide strong cryptographic strength against potential attacks.

The GUI is thoughtfully designed with two main tabs: "Generate Keys" and "View Keys". The "Generate Keys" tab contains a descriptive label and a button labeled "Generate DSA Keys." When the user clicks this button, the application invokes the generate_keys method, which utilizes the dsa.generate_private_key function to create a private key and subsequently derives the corresponding public key. These keys are then serialized into PEM (Privacy Enhanced Mail) format using the serialization module, allowing them to be easily stored or transmitted. The serialized keys are displayed in scrollable text areas within the "View Keys" tab, providing users with a clear and organized view of their newly generated keys. Additionally, the interface includes buttons to save each key to a file, enhancing the application's practicality by enabling users to securely store their keys for future use.

Functionality-wise, the application incorporates robust features to ensure a seamless user experience. Upon generating the keys, the private and public keys are displayed in separate scrollable text boxes, allowing users to review and verify the generated content immediately. The "Save Private Key" and "Save Public Key" buttons facilitate the export of these keys to .pem files, utilizing file dialogs to let users choose their desired save locations and filenames. Error handling is meticulously implemented through try-except blocks, ensuring that any issues encountered during key generation or file saving are gracefully managed with informative error messages displayed via message boxes. Success notifications further enhance user feedback, confirming the successful completion of actions such as key generation and file saving. Overall, this project delivers a rich, interactive, and secure application that simplifies the complexities of DSA key management, making it an invaluable tool for developers, security professionals, and anyone interested in digital cryptography.

```python
import tkinter as tk
from tkinter import ttk, scrolledtext, filedialog, messagebox
from cryptography.hazmat.primitives.asymmetric import dsa
from cryptography.hazmat.primitives import serialization

class DSAKeyGeneratorApp:
    def __init__(self, root):
        self.root = root
        self.root.title("DSA Key Generator")
        self.root.geometry("800x600")
        self.create_widgets()

    def create_widgets(self):
        # Create Tab control
        tab_control = ttk.Notebook(self.root)

        # Tab 1 - Key Generation
        tab_generate = ttk.Frame(tab_control)
        tab_control.add(tab_generate, text="Generate Keys")

        # Tab 2 - Display Keys
        tab_display = ttk.Frame(tab_control)
        tab_control.add(tab_display, text="View Keys")

        # Add Tabs to the window
        tab_control.pack(expand=1, fill="both")

        # Key Generation Tab
        ttk.Label(tab_generate, text="Click 'Generate DSA Keys' to create a new pair of DSA keys.").grid(column=0, row=0, padx=10, pady=10)
        self.generate_button = ttk.Button(tab_generate, text="Generate DSA Keys", command=self.generate_keys)
        self.generate_button.grid(column=0, row=1, padx=10, pady=10)

        # Text boxes for generated keys
        self.private_key_display = scrolledtext.ScrolledText(tab_display, wrap=tk.WORD, width=80, height=10)
        self.private_key_display.grid(column=0, row=1, padx=10, pady=10)
        self.public_key_display = scrolledtext.ScrolledText(tab_display, wrap=tk.WORD, width=80, height=10)
        self.public_key_display.grid(column=0, row=3, padx=10, pady=10)

        # Labels for the keys
        ttk.Label(tab_display, text="DSA Private Key:").grid(column=0, row=0, padx=10, pady=5)
        ttk.Label(tab_display, text="DSA Public Key:").grid(column=0, row=2, padx=10, pady=5)

        # Save buttons for keys
        ttk.Button(tab_display, text="Save Private Key", command=self.save_private_key).grid(column=0, row=5, padx=10, pady=5)
        ttk.Button(tab_display, text="Save Public Key", command=self.save_public_key).grid(column=0, row=6, padx=10, pady=5)

    def generate_keys(self):
        try:
            # Generate DSA keys
            self.private_key = dsa.generate_private_key(key_size=2048)
            self.public_key = self.private_key.public_key()

            # Serialize the private key to PEM format
            self.private_pem = self.private_key.private_bytes(
                encoding=serialization.Encoding.PEM,
                format=serialization.PrivateFormat.TraditionalOpenSSL,
                encryption_algorithm=serialization.NoEncryption()
            )
```

```python
            # Serialize the public key to PEM format
            self.public_pem = self.public_key.public_bytes(
                encoding=serialization.Encoding.PEM,
                format=serialization.PublicFormat.SubjectPublicKeyInfo
            )

            # Display the keys in the text boxes
            self.private_key_display.delete(1.0, tk.END)
            self.private_key_display.insert(tk.INSERT, self.private_pem.decode())

            self.public_key_display.delete(1.0, tk.END)
            self.public_key_display.insert(tk.INSERT, self.public_pem.decode())

            messagebox.showinfo("Success", "DSA keys generated successfully!")

        except Exception as e:
            messagebox.showerror("Error", f"An error occurred: {e}")

    def save_private_key(self):
        try:
            file_path = filedialog.asksaveasfilename(defaultextension=".pem", filetypes=[("PEM Files", "*.pem")])
            if file_path:
                with open(file_path, "wb") as file:
                    file.write(self.private_pem)
                messagebox.showinfo("Success", "Private key saved successfully!")
        except Exception as e:
            messagebox.showerror("Error", f"Could not save private key: {e}")

    def save_public_key(self):
        try:
            file_path = filedialog.asksaveasfilename(defaultextension=".pem", filetypes=[("PEM Files", "*.pem")])
            if file_path:
                with open(file_path, "wb") as file:
                    file.write(self.public_pem)
                messagebox.showinfo("Success", "Public key saved successfully!")
        except Exception as e:
            messagebox.showerror("Error", f"Could not save public key: {e}")

if __name__ == "__main__":
    root = tk.Tk()
    app = DSAKeyGeneratorApp(root)
    root.mainloop()
```

This code is a Digital Signature Algorithm (DSA) Key Generator application with a graphical user interface (GUI) built using Python's tkinter library. It allows users to generate, view, and save DSA private and public keys. Here's the explanation of each part:

Importing Libraries

```
import tkinter as tk
from tkinter import ttk, scrolledtext, filedialog, messagebox
from cryptography.hazmat.primitives.asymmetric import dsa
from cryptography.hazmat.primitives import serialization
```

- tkinter and ttk: These are Python's standard GUI libraries. tkinter is used to create windows and widgets, while ttk provides themed widgets like Notebook, Button, and Label.
- scrolledtext: This widget allows a text box with a scrollbar, which is useful when displaying large text, such as the generated keys.
- filedialog: This module provides dialog boxes that allow the user to select a file or directory.
- messagebox: This module displays pop-up messages like errors or information.
- dsa from cryptography.hazmat: This module provides DSA (Digital Signature Algorithm) functionality to generate asymmetric keys.
- serialization: This module serializes and deserializes the DSA keys into formats like PEM (Privacy Enhanced Mail), which can be saved or transmitted securely.

Class DSAKeyGeneratorApp and Initialization

```
class DSAKeyGeneratorApp:
    def __init__(self, root):
        self.root = root
        self.root.title("DSA Key Generator")
        self.root.geometry("800x600")
        self.create_widgets()
```

- __init__ method: This is the constructor that initializes the application. It sets the window's title to "DSA Key Generator" and its size to 800x600 pixels.
- create_widgets method: This method is called inside the constructor to create all the widgets (buttons, text boxes, labels, etc.) in the GUI.

Creating Tabs

```
def create_widgets(self):
    tab_control = ttk.Notebook(self.root)

    tab_generate = ttk.Frame(tab_control)
    tab_control.add(tab_generate, text="Generate Keys")

    tab_display = ttk.Frame(tab_control)
    tab_control.add(tab_display, text="View Keys")

    tab_control.pack(expand=1, fill="both")
```

- ttk.Notebook: This widget creates a tabbed interface. Two tabs are created:

- "Generate Keys" tab: Contains a button to generate DSA keys.
- "View Keys" tab: Displays the generated private and public keys in separate scrollable text boxes.
- tab_control.pack(expand=1, fill="both"): This command expands the tab control to fill the window.

Key Generation Tab Widgets

```
ttk.Label(tab_generate, text="Click 'Generate DSA Keys' to create a new pair of DSA
keys.").grid(column=0, row=0, padx=10, pady=10)
self.generate_button = ttk.Button(tab_generate, text="Generate DSA Keys",
command=self.generate_keys)
self.generate_button.grid(column=0, row=1, padx=10, pady=10)
```

- ttk.Label: Adds a label to instruct the user to click the button to generate keys.
- ttk.Button: Adds a button that, when clicked, calls the generate_keys method to generate the DSA keys.

Display Keys Tab Widgets

```
self.private_key_display = scrolledtext.ScrolledText(tab_display, wrap=tk.WORD,
width=80, height=10)
self.private_key_display.grid(column=0, row=1, padx=10, pady=10)
self.public_key_display = scrolledtext.ScrolledText(tab_display, wrap=tk.WORD,
width=80, height=10)
self.public_key_display.grid(column=0, row=3, padx=10, pady=10)
```

- ScrolledText: These widgets display the generated private and public keys in scrollable text boxes. The text is wrapped by words, and the box is set to 80 characters wide and 10 lines tall.
- Grid method: Positions the text boxes and labels in the tab using a grid layout.

Key Generation Logic

```
def generate_keys(self):
    try:
        self.private_key = dsa.generate_private_key(key_size=2048)
        self.public_key = self.private_key.public_key()
        
        self.private_pem = self.private_key.private_bytes(
            encoding=serialization.Encoding.PEM,
```

```
            format=serialization.PrivateFormat.TraditionalOpenSSL,
            encryption_algorithm=serialization.NoEncryption()
        )

        self.public_pem = self.public_key.public_bytes(
            encoding=serialization.Encoding.PEM,
            format=serialization.PublicFormat.SubjectPublicKeyInfo
        )

        self.private_key_display.delete(1.0, tk.END)
        self.private_key_display.insert(tk.INSERT, self.private_pem.decode())
        self.public_key_display.delete(1.0, tk.END)
        self.public_key_display.insert(tk.INSERT, self.public_pem.decode())

        messagebox.showinfo("Success", "DSA keys generated successfully!")
    except Exception as e:
        messagebox.showerror("Error", f"An error occurred: {e}")
```

- generate_keys method: This is triggered when the "Generate DSA Keys" button is clicked.
    - dsa.generate_private_key(key_size=2048): Generates a DSA private key with a key size of 2048 bits.
    - self.private_key.private_bytes and self.public_key.public_bytes: These methods serialize the private and public keys into PEM format.
    - Display in Text Boxes: The text boxes are cleared and then populated with the serialized private and public keys using the insert method.
    - Error handling: If an error occurs during key generation, it is caught, and an error message is shown in a message box.

Saving Keys to File

```
def save_private_key(self):
    try:
        file_path = filedialog.asksaveasfilename(defaultextension=".pem",
filetypes=[("PEM Files", "*.pem")])
        if file_path:
            with open(file_path, "wb") as file:
                file.write(self.private_pem)
        messagebox.showinfo("Success", "Private key saved successfully!")
    except Exception as e:
        messagebox.showerror("Error", f"Could not save private key: {e}")

def save_public_key(self):
    try:
        file_path = filedialog.asksaveasfilename(defaultextension=".pem",
filetypes=[("PEM Files", "*.pem")])
        if file_path:
            with open(file_path, "wb") as file:
```

```
        file.write(self.public_pem)
    messagebox.showinfo("Success", "Public key saved successfully!")
except Exception as e:
    messagebox.showerror("Error", f"Could not save public key: {e}")
```

- save_private_key and save_public_key: These methods open a file dialog to let the user select a location to save the private and public keys as .pem files. The keys are written to the file in binary mode (wb).
- Error handling: If saving fails, an error message is displayed in a message box.

Main Program Execution

```
if __name__ == "__main__":
    root = tk.Tk()
    app = DSAKeyGeneratorApp(root)
    root.mainloop()
```

- root = tk.Tk(): Creates the main application window.
- app = DSAKeyGeneratorApp(root): Initializes the DSAKeyGeneratorApp class, passing the root window.
- root.mainloop(): Starts the tkinter event loop, allowing the GUI to function.

SIGNING AND VERIFYING SIGNATURER
Project 3: Signing and Verifying DSA Signature

This code demonstrates the process of signing and verifying a message using the Digital Signature Algorithm (DSA) in Python, while ensuring the signature is UTF-8 safe by encoding it in Base64. It begins by generating a DSA private and public key pair with a key size of 2048 bits. A message (in bytes) is then created, which is the data to be signed. The private key is used to generate a digital signature for the message using the SHA-256 hashing algorithm, ensuring the integrity and authenticity of the message. The generated signature, which is binary data, is encoded into Base64 format to make it text-safe and suitable for UTF-8 encoding.

To verify the signature, the Base64-encoded signature is first decoded back into its original binary form. The public key is then used to verify the authenticity of the signature by comparing it to the message. If the verification is successful, the message "Signature is valid." is printed; otherwise, an InvalidSignature exception is raised, and the message "Signature is invalid." is displayed. This approach ensures that the digital signature can be safely transmitted or stored as text without data corruption, while still preserving its security properties.

```python
import base64
from cryptography.hazmat.primitives.asymmetric import dsa
from cryptography.hazmat.primitives import hashes
from cryptography.exceptions import InvalidSignature

# Step 1: Generate DSA private and public keys
private_key = dsa.generate_private_key(key_size=2048)
public_key = private_key.public_key()

# Step 2: Create a message to sign
message = b"Important message to be signed."

# Step 3: Sign the message using the private key
signature = private_key.sign(
    message,
    hashes.SHA256()
)

# Step 4: Encode the binary signature to a Base64 string (UTF-8 safe)
signature_base64 = base64.b64encode(signature).decode('utf-8')
print("Signature (Base64, UTF-8 safe):", signature_base64)

# Step 5: Decode Base64 back to binary for verification
signature_bytes = base64.b64decode(signature_base64)

# Step 6: Verify the signature using the public key
try:
```

```
        public_key.verify(
            signature_bytes,   # Use the decoded binary signature
            message,
            hashes.SHA256()
        )
    print("Signature is valid.")
except InvalidSignature:
    print("Signature is invalid.")
```

Here's the breakdown of each part of the code:

Import Libraries:

```
import base64
from cryptography.hazmat.primitives.asymmetric import dsa
from cryptography.hazmat.primitives import hashes
from cryptography.exceptions import InvalidSignature
```

- This section imports the necessary modules. base64 is used for encoding and decoding the signature in Base64 format. dsa is from the cryptography library and provides the implementation of the Digital Signature Algorithm. hashes provides cryptographic hash functions, and InvalidSignature is an exception class used to handle verification failures.

Generate DSA Private and Public Keys:

```
private_key = dsa.generate_private_key(key_size=2048)
public_key = private_key.public_key()
```

- Here, a DSA private key is generated with a key size of 2048 bits. This private key is then used to derive the corresponding public key. The private key is used for signing messages, while the public key is used for verifying the signatures.

Create a Message to Sign:

```
message = b"Important message to be signed."
```

- A message (a byte string) is defined. This is the data that will be signed. The message is in bytes format because cryptographic operations typically work with byte data rather than text strings.

Sign the Message Using the Private Key:

```
signature = private_key.sign(
    message,
    hashes.SHA256()
)
```

- The sign() method of the private key is used to create a digital signature for the message. The SHA-256 hash function is specified for this operation, ensuring that the message is hashed with SHA-256 before signing. The result is a digital signature in binary format.

Encode the Binary Signature to Base64 (UTF-8 Safe):

```
signature_base64 = base64.b64encode(signature).decode('utf-8')
print("Signature (Base64, UTF-8 safe):", signature_base64)
```

- The binary signature is encoded into Base64 format using base64.b64encode(). Base64 encoding converts binary data into a text representation that is UTF-8 safe, meaning it can be easily stored or transmitted as text. The .decode('utf-8') method converts the Base64 bytes into a UTF-8 string for display purposes.

Decode Base64 Back to Binary for Verification:

```
signature_bytes = base64.b64decode(signature_base64)
```

- The Base64-encoded signature is decoded back into its original binary form using base64.b64decode(). This step is necessary to convert the text representation back into a format that can be used for verification.

Verify the Signature Using the Public Key:

```
try:
    public_key.verify(
        signature_bytes,   # Use the decoded binary signature
        message,
        hashes.SHA256()
    )
    print("Signature is valid.")
except InvalidSignature:
```

```
print("Signature is invalid.")
```

- The verify() method of the public key is used to check the validity of the signature. It compares the provided signature against the message and ensures it was created with the corresponding private key and SHA-256 hash function. If the verification is successful, it prints "Signature is valid." If the signature does not match, it raises an InvalidSignature exception, and "Signature is invalid." is printed. This step confirms that the signature is authentic and the message has not been tampered with.

Project 4: GUI Tkinter for Signing and Verifying DSA Signature

The project is a comprehensive Tkinter-based graphical user interface (GUI) application designed for Digital Signature Algorithm (DSA) operations. It provides users with an intuitive interface to generate DSA keys, sign messages, and verify signatures. The application consists of two main tabs: one for key generation and another for signing and verification tasks. The key generation tab allows users to generate a pair of DSA keys, displaying both private and public keys in PEM format within scrollable text areas. This feature helps in managing large key data without requiring excessive scrolling.

The second tab focuses on signing and verifying messages. Users can input a message, sign it using the generated private key, and view the Base64-encoded signature. The application provides a text box for displaying the encoded signature, ensuring it is easily readable and copyable. The "Sign Message" button triggers the signing process, while the "Verify Signature" button is used to check the validity of the signature against the original message using the public key. This functionality helps users verify the authenticity and integrity of signed messages.

The application is designed to handle errors gracefully, using message boxes to provide feedback on the success or failure of various operations. For instance, if key generation or signing operations fail, the application will display an error message detailing the issue. This robustness ensures that users can effectively interact with the cryptographic functions without encountering unhandled exceptions. Overall, the DSAKeyApp project demonstrates a practical and user-friendly approach to cryptographic operations, integrating key management and message signing/verification into a single, accessible tool.

```python
import tkinter as tk
from tkinter import ttk, scrolledtext, messagebox
import base64
from cryptography.hazmat.primitives.asymmetric import dsa
from cryptography.hazmat.primitives import hashes, serialization
from cryptography.exceptions import InvalidSignature

class DSAKeyApp:
    def __init__(self, root):
        self.root = root
        self.root.title("DSA Signing and Verification")
        self.root.geometry("800x600")
        self.create_widgets()

    def create_widgets(self):
        # Create Tab control
        tab_control = ttk.Notebook(self.root)

        # Tab 1 - Key Generation
        tab_keygen = ttk.Frame(tab_control)
        tab_control.add(tab_keygen, text="Key Generation")

        # Tab 2 - Sign and Verify
        tab_sign_verify = ttk.Frame(tab_control)
        tab_control.add(tab_sign_verify, text="Sign and Verify")

        # Add Tabs to the window
        tab_control.pack(expand=1, fill="both")

        # Key Generation Tab
        ttk.Label(tab_keygen, text="Generate DSA Keys:").grid(column=0, row=0, padx=10, pady=10)
        ttk.Button(tab_keygen, text="Generate Keys", command=self.generate_keys).grid(column=0, row=1, padx=10, pady=10)

        ttk.Label(tab_keygen, text="Private Key:").grid(column=0, row=2, padx=10, pady=5)
        self.private_key_display = scrolledtext.ScrolledText(tab_keygen, wrap=tk.WORD, width=80, height=10)
        self.private_key_display.grid(column=0, row=3, padx=10, pady=10)

        ttk.Label(tab_keygen, text="Public Key:").grid(column=0, row=4, padx=10, pady=5)
        self.public_key_display = scrolledtext.ScrolledText(tab_keygen, wrap=tk.WORD, width=80, height=10)
        self.public_key_display.grid(column=0, row=5, padx=10, pady=10)

        # Sign and Verify Tab
        ttk.Label(tab_sign_verify, text="Message:").grid(column=0, row=0, padx=10, pady=5)
        self.message_entry = tk.Entry(tab_sign_verify, width=80)
        self.message_entry.grid(column=0, row=1, padx=10, pady=5)

        ttk.Button(tab_sign_verify, text="Sign Message", command=self.sign_message).grid(column=0, row=2, padx=10, pady=10)

        ttk.Label(tab_sign_verify, text="Signature (Base64):").grid(column=0, row=3, padx=10, pady=5)
```

```python
        self.signature_display = scrolledtext.ScrolledText(tab_sign_verify, 
wrap=tk.WORD, width=80, height=10)
        self.signature_display.grid(column=0, row=4, padx=10, pady=10)

        ttk.Button(tab_sign_verify, text="Verify Signature", 
command=self.verify_signature).grid(column=0, row=5, padx=10, pady=10)

    def generate_keys(self):
        try:
            # Generate DSA keys
            self.private_key = dsa.generate_private_key(key_size=2048)
            self.public_key = self.private_key.public_key()

            # Serialize keys to PEM format
            self.private_pem = self.private_key.private_bytes(
                encoding=serialization.Encoding.PEM,
                format=serialization.PrivateFormat.TraditionalOpenSSL,
                encryption_algorithm=serialization.NoEncryption()
            )

            self.public_pem = self.public_key.public_bytes(
                encoding=serialization.Encoding.PEM,
                format=serialization.PublicFormat.SubjectPublicKeyInfo
            )

            # Display keys in the text boxes
            self.private_key_display.delete(1.0, tk.END)
            self.private_key_display.insert(tk.INSERT, self.private_pem.decode())

            self.public_key_display.delete(1.0, tk.END)
            self.public_key_display.insert(tk.INSERT, self.public_pem.decode())

            messagebox.showinfo("Success", "DSA keys generated successfully!")
        except Exception as e:
            messagebox.showerror("Error", f"An error occurred: {e}")

    def sign_message(self):
        try:
            # Retrieve the message from the entry widget
            message = self.message_entry.get().encode('utf-8')

            # Sign the message
            signature = self.private_key.sign(
                message,
                hashes.SHA256()
            )

            # Encode the signature to Base64
            self.signature_base64 = base64.b64encode(signature).decode('utf-8')

            # Display the Base64 encoded signature
            self.signature_display.delete(1.0, tk.END)
            self.signature_display.insert(tk.INSERT, self.signature_base64)

            messagebox.showinfo("Success", "Message signed successfully!")
        except Exception as e:
            messagebox.showerror("Error", f"An error occurred: {e}")
```

```
    def verify_signature(self):
        try:
            # Retrieve the message and signature from the widgets
            message = self.message_entry.get().encode('utf-8')
            signature_bytes = base64.b64decode(self.signature_base64)

            # Verify the signature
            self.public_key.verify(
                signature_bytes,
                message,
                hashes.SHA256()
            )

            messagebox.showinfo("Success", "Signature is valid.")
        except InvalidSignature:
            messagebox.showerror("Error", "Signature is invalid.")
        except Exception as e:
            messagebox.showerror("Error", f"An error occurred: {e}")

if __name__ == "__main__":
    root = tk.Tk()
    app = DSAKeyApp(root)
    root.mainloop()
```

Here's the explanation of each part of the code for creating a Tkinter GUI application that handles DSA key generation, message signing, and signature verification.

Imports and Class Definition

```
import tkinter as tk
from tkinter import ttk, scrolledtext, messagebox
import base64
from cryptography.hazmat.primitives.asymmetric import dsa
from cryptography.hazmat.primitives import hashes, serialization
from cryptography.exceptions import InvalidSignature
```

- import tkinter as tk: Imports the Tkinter module, used for creating the graphical user interface (GUI).
- from tkinter import ttk, scrolledtext, messagebox: Imports specific Tkinter submodules:
  - ttk: Provides themed widgets that are more modern than the standard Tkinter widgets.
  - scrolledtext: Allows the creation of a text widget with scrollbars, useful for displaying large amounts of text.
  - messagebox: Provides functions to display popup messages to the user.
- import base64: Imports the base64 module for encoding and decoding data in Base64 format.

- from cryptography.hazmat.primitives.asymmetric import dsa: Imports the DSA (Digital Signature Algorithm) class from the cryptography library, used for generating and managing DSA keys.
- from cryptography.hazmat.primitives import hashes, serialization: Imports cryptographic hash functions and serialization utilities:
  - hashes: Provides hashing algorithms like SHA256.
  - serialization: Helps in converting cryptographic keys to and from different formats.
- from cryptography.exceptions import InvalidSignature: Imports the InvalidSignature exception to handle cases where a signature verification fails.

Class Initialization and Main Window Setup

```
class DSAKeyApp:
    def __init__(self, root):
        self.root = root
        self.root.title("DSA Signing and Verification")
        self.root.geometry("800x600")
        self.create_widgets()
```

- class DSAKeyApp: Defines a class for the application, encapsulating all functionalities related to DSA operations.
- def __init__(self, root):: Initializes the DSAKeyApp class. This method is called when an instance of the class is created.
  - self.root = root: Stores the reference to the main Tkinter window in self.root.
  - self.root.title("DSA Signing and Verification"): Sets the title of the main window.
  - self.root.geometry("800x600"): Sets the initial size of the window to 800x600 pixels.
  - self.create_widgets(): Calls a method to create and arrange the GUI components.

Widget Creation and Layout

```
def create_widgets(self):
    # Create Tab control
    tab_control = ttk.Notebook(self.root)
```

- def create_widgets(self):: Defines a method for creating and arranging all GUI components.
- tab_control = ttk.Notebook(self.root): Creates a Notebook widget, which allows for tabbed interfaces within the main window.

Key Generation Tab

```
# Tab 1 - Key Generation
tab_keygen = ttk.Frame(tab_control)
tab_control.add(tab_keygen, text="Key Generation")
```

- tab_keygen = ttk.Frame(tab_control): Creates a frame widget that will act as the content area for the "Key Generation" tab.
- tab_control.add(tab_keygen, text="Key Generation"): Adds the frame as a tab to the Notebook with the label "Key Generation".

```
ttk.Label(tab_keygen, text="Generate DSA Keys:").grid(column=0, row=0, padx=10, pady=10)
    ttk.Button(tab_keygen, text="Generate Keys", command=self.generate_keys).grid(column=0, row=1, padx=10, pady=10)
```

- ttk.Label(tab_keygen, text="Generate DSA Keys:"): Adds a label prompting the user to generate DSA keys.
- .grid(column=0, row=0, padx=10, pady=10): Positions the label in the grid layout of the tab_keygen frame with padding.
- ttk.Button(tab_keygen, text="Generate Keys", command=self.generate_keys): Adds a button to generate DSA keys. The command parameter links the button to the generate_keys method.
- .grid(column=0, row=1, padx=10, pady=10): Positions the button below the label with padding.

```
ttk.Label(tab_keygen, text="Private Key:").grid(column=0, row=2, padx=10, pady=5)
    self.private_key_display = scrolledtext.ScrolledText(tab_keygen, wrap=tk.WORD, width=80, height=10)
    self.private_key_display.grid(column=0, row=3, padx=10, pady=10)

    ttk.Label(tab_keygen, text="Public Key:").grid(column=0, row=4, padx=10, pady=5)
    self.public_key_display = scrolledtext.ScrolledText(tab_keygen, wrap=tk.WORD, width=80, height=10)
    self.public_key_display.grid(column=0, row=5, padx=10, pady=10)
```

- ttk.Label(tab_keygen, text="Private Key:"): Adds a label to indicate where the private key will be displayed.
- self.private_key_display = scrolledtext.ScrolledText(tab_keygen, wrap=tk.WORD, width=80, height=10): Creates a ScrolledText widget for displaying the private key. The wrap=tk.WORD ensures that text wraps at word boundaries.
- .grid(column=0, row=3, padx=10, pady=10): Positions the ScrolledText widget below the "Private Key" label.
- ttk.Label(tab_keygen, text="Public Key:"): Adds a label for the public key display.
- self.public_key_display = scrolledtext.ScrolledText(tab_keygen, wrap=tk.WORD, width=80, height=10): Creates a ScrolledText widget for the public key, with similar properties as the private key display.
- .grid(column=0, row=5, padx=10, pady=10): Positions the public key display below the corresponding label.

Sign and Verify Tab

```
# Tab 2 - Sign and Verify
tab_sign_verify = ttk.Frame(tab_control)
tab_control.add(tab_sign_verify, text="Sign and Verify")
```

- tab_sign_verify = ttk.Frame(tab_control): Creates a frame for the "Sign and Verify" tab.
- tab_control.add(tab_sign_verify, text="Sign and Verify"): Adds this frame as a new tab with the label "Sign and Verify".

```
    ttk.Label(tab_sign_verify, text="Message:").grid(column=0, row=0, padx=10, pady=5)
    self.message_entry = tk.Entry(tab_sign_verify, width=80)
    self.message_entry.grid(column=0, row=1, padx=10, pady=5)
```

- ttk.Label(tab_sign_verify, text="Message:"): Adds a label prompting the user to enter a message.
- self.message_entry = tk.Entry(tab_sign_verify, width=80): Creates an entry widget where users can input the message to be signed.
- .grid(column=0, row=1, padx=10, pady=5): Positions the entry widget below the message label.

```
    ttk.Button(tab_sign_verify, text="Sign Message",
command=self.sign_message).grid(column=0, row=2, padx=10, pady=10)
```

- ttk.Button(tab_sign_verify, text="Sign Message", command=self.sign_message): Adds a button for signing the entered message. The command parameter links the button to the sign_message method.
- .grid(column=0, row=2, padx=10, pady=10): Positions the button below the message entry widget.

```
    ttk.Label(tab_sign_verify, text="Signature (Base64):").grid(column=0, row=3,
padx=10, pady=5)
    self.signature_display = scrolledtext.ScrolledText(tab_sign_verify, wrap=tk.WORD,
width=80, height=10)
    self.signature_display.grid(column=0, row=4, padx=10, pady=10)

    ttk.Button(tab_sign_verify, text="Verify Signature",
command=self.verify_signature).grid(column=0, row=5, padx=10, pady=10)
```

- ttk.Label(tab_sign_verify, text="Signature (Base64):"): Adds a label indicating where the Base64-encoded signature will be displayed.
- self.signature_display = scrolledtext.ScrolledText(tab_sign_verify, wrap=tk.WORD, width=80, height=10): Creates a ScrolledText widget for displaying the Base64 signature.
- .grid(column=0, row=4, padx=10, pady=10): Positions the ScrolledText widget below the signature label.
- ttk.Button(tab_sign_verify, text="Verify Signature", command=self.verify_signature): Adds a button for verifying the signature. The command parameter links the button to the verify_signature method.
- .grid(column=0, row=5, padx=10, pady=10): Positions the verification button below the signature display.

Key Generation Method

```
def generate_keys(self):
    private_key = dsa.generate_private_key(key_size=2048)
    public_key = private_key.public_key()

    private_pem = private_key.private_bytes(
        encoding=serialization.Encoding.PEM,
        format=serialization.PrivateFormat.PKCS8,
```

```
        encryption_algorithm=serialization.NoEncryption()
    )
    public_pem = public_key.public_bytes(
        encoding=serialization.Encoding.PEM,
        format=serialization.PublicFormat.SubjectPublicKeyInfo
    )
    self.private_key_display.delete(1.0, tk.END)
    self.private_key_display.insert(tk.END, private_pem.decode('utf-8'))

    self.public_key_display.delete(1.0, tk.END)
    self.public_key_display.insert(tk.END, public_pem.decode('utf-8'))
```

- def generate_keys(self):: Defines the method to generate DSA keys.
- private_key = dsa.generate_private_key(key_size=2048): Generates a new DSA private key with a size of 2048 bits.
- public_key = private_key.public_key(): Derives the corresponding public key from the private key.
- private_pem = private_key.private_bytes(...): Serializes the private key to PEM format without encryption.
- public_pem = public_key.public_bytes(...): Serializes the public key to PEM format.
- self.private_key_display.delete(1.0, tk.END): Clears any existing text in the private key display widget.
- self.private_key_display.insert(tk.END, private_pem.decode('utf-8')): Inserts the private key PEM data into the display widget.
- self.public_key_display.delete(1.0, tk.END): Clears any existing text in the public key display widget.
- self.public_key_display.insert(tk.END, public_pem.decode('utf-8')): Inserts the public key PEM data into the display widget.

Message Signing Method

```
def sign_message(self):
    message = self.message_entry.get()
    if not message:
        messagebox.showerror("Error", "Message cannot be empty!")
        return

    try:
        private_key = serialization.load_pem_private_key(
            self.private_key_display.get(1.0, tk.END).encode('utf-8'),
            password=None
```

```
    )
    signature = private_key.sign(
        message.encode('utf-8'),
        padding=dsapads.PKCS1v15(),
        algorithm=hashes.SHA256()
    )
    signature_base64 = base64.b64encode(signature).decode('utf-8')

    self.signature_display.delete(1.0, tk.END)
    self.signature_display.insert(tk.END, signature_base64)
except Exception as e:
    messagebox.showerror("Error", str(e))
```

- def sign_message(self):: Defines the method to sign a message.
- message = self.message_entry.get(): Retrieves the message entered by the user.
- if not message:: Checks if the message is empty.
- messagebox.showerror("Error", "Message cannot be empty!"): Displays an error message if the message is empty.
- private_key = serialization.load_pem_private_key(...): Loads the private key from PEM format. Note that dsapads needs to be defined or imported if used.
- signature = private_key.sign(...): Signs the message using the private key.
- signature_base64 = base64.b64encode(signature).decode('utf-8'): Encodes the signature in Base64 format.
- self.signature_display.delete(1.0, tk.END): Clears any existing text in the signature display widget.
- self.signature_display.insert(tk.END, signature_base64): Inserts the Base64-encoded signature into the display widget.

Signature Verification Method

```
def verify_signature(self):
    message = self.message_entry.get()
    signature_base64 = self.signature_display.get(1.0, tk.END).strip()
    if not message or not signature_base64:
        messagebox.showerror("Error", "Message and Signature cannot be empty!")
        return

    try:
        public_key = serialization.load_pem_public_key(
            self.public_key_display.get(1.0, tk.END).encode('utf-8')
        )
        signature = base64.b64decode(signature_base64)
        public_key.verify(
            signature,
            message.encode('utf-8'),
```

```
            padding=dsapads.PKCS1v15(),
            algorithm=hashes.SHA256()
        )
        messagebox.showinfo("Success", "Signature is valid!")
    except InvalidSignature:
        messagebox.showerror("Error", "Invalid signature!")
    except Exception as e:
        messagebox.showerror("Error", str(e))
```

- def verify_signature(self):: Defines the method to verify a signature.
- message = self.message_entry.get(): Retrieves the message from the entry widget.
- signature_base64 = self.signature_display.get(1.0, tk.END).strip(): Retrieves and strips any extra whitespace from the Base64 signature.
- if not message or not signature_base64:: Checks if the message or signature is empty.
- messagebox.showerror("Error", "Message and Signature cannot be empty!"): Displays an error message if either is empty.
- public_key = serialization.load_pem_public_key(...): Loads the public key from PEM format.
- signature = base64.b64decode(signature_base64): Decodes the Base64 signature.
- public_key.verify(...): Verifies the signature against the message using the public key.
- messagebox.showinfo("Success", "Signature is valid!"): Displays a success message if the signature is valid.
- except InvalidSignature:: Catches signature verification errors.
- messagebox.showerror("Error", "Invalid signature!"): Displays an error message if the signature is invalid.
- except Exception as e:: Catches other exceptions.
- messagebox.showerror("Error", str(e)): Displays an error message for other exceptions.

Main Function to Run the Application

```
def main():
    root = tk.Tk()
    app = DSAKeyApp(root)
    root.mainloop()

if __name__ == "__main__":
    main()
```

- def main():: Defines the main function to set up and run the application.
- root = tk.Tk(): Creates the main Tkinter window.
- app = DSAKeyApp(root): Creates an instance of DSAKeyApp, passing the main window as an argument.
- root.mainloop(): Starts the Tkinter event loop, allowing the GUI to respond to user interactions.
- if __name__ == "__main__":: Ensures that main() is called only if the script is run directly (not imported as a module).

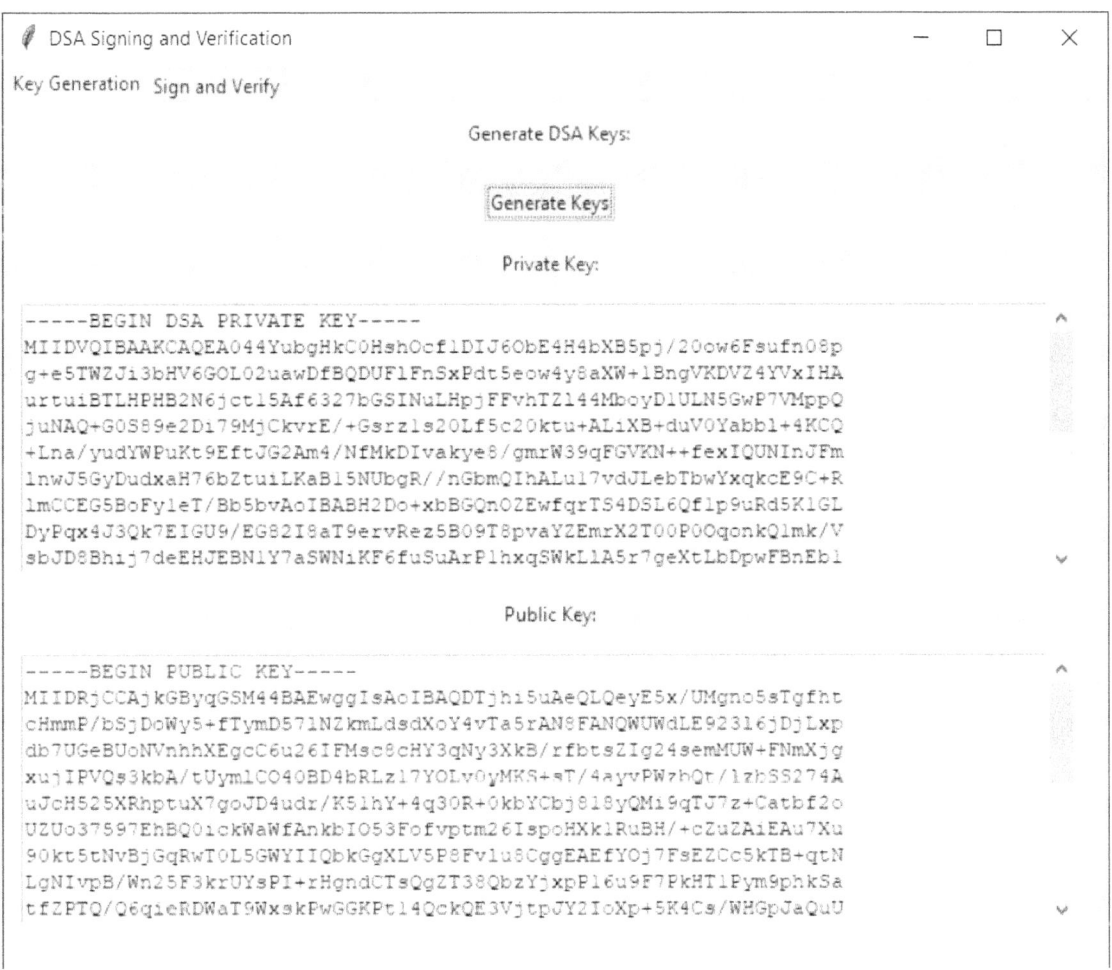

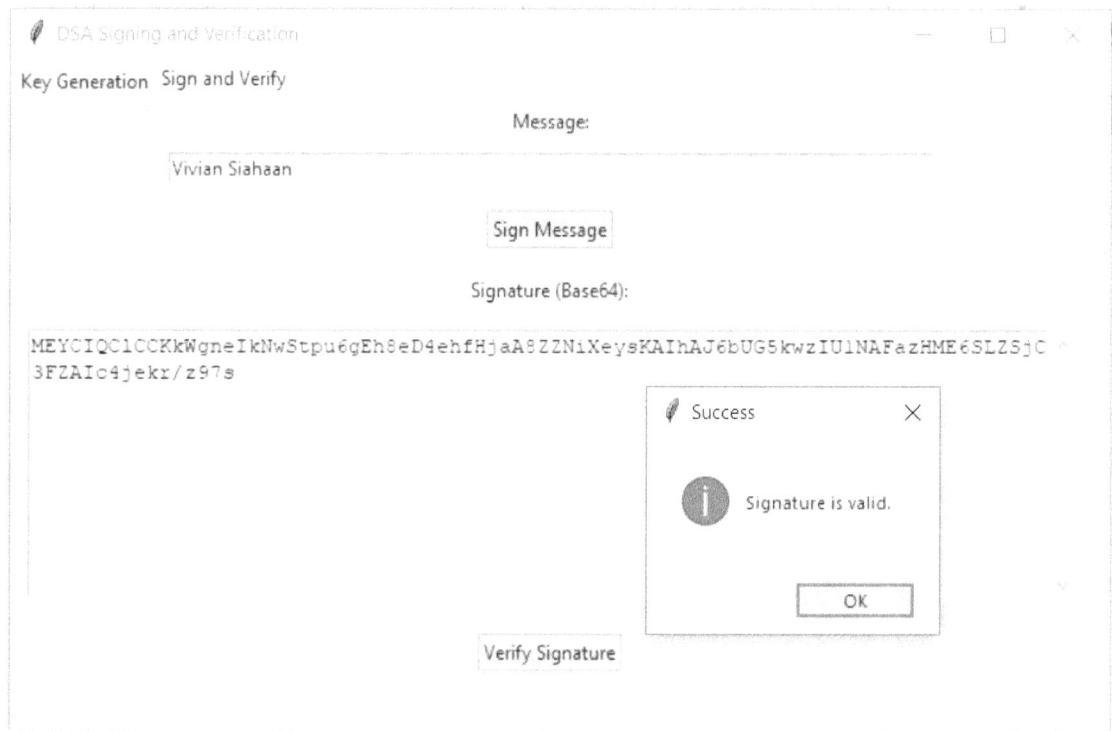

REAL-WORLD EXAMPLES
Project 5: Signing and Verifying File

The code is a complete implementation for generating, signing, and verifying files using the DSA (Digital Signature Algorithm). It consists of several functions and a main block that orchestrates the entire process. The generate_and_save_keys() function creates a pair of DSA keys (private and public), serializes them to PEM format, and saves them to files. This function prints the keys in PEM format to the console to provide immediate visibility of the generated keys.

The sign_file() function takes the private key, reads a file's content, hashes it using SHA-256, and then signs this hash with the private key. The resulting signature is saved to a file and also printed in its Base64-encoded form for easier readability. This step ensures that the file's content can be uniquely identified and verified later using its signature.

The verify_file_signature function loads the public key, reads the file content and its signature, and then hashes the file content. It attempts to verify the signature against this hash using the public key. The function prints the signature (Base64-encoded) and confirms whether the signature is valid or not, providing error messages if the verification fails. The main function coordinates the process by calling these functions in sequence, including checking for the existence of a test file and creating it if necessary.

```python
import os
import hashlib
import base64
from cryptography.hazmat.primitives.asymmetric import dsa
from cryptography.hazmat.primitives import hashes, serialization
from cryptography.exceptions import InvalidSignature

# Function to generate and save DSA keys
def generate_and_save_keys(private_key_path, public_key_path):
    # Generate a private key
    private_key = dsa.generate_private_key(key_size=2048)

    # Derive the public key
    public_key = private_key.public_key()

    # Serialize the private key to PEM format
    private_pem = private_key.private_bytes(
        encoding=serialization.Encoding.PEM,
        format=serialization.PrivateFormat.PKCS8,
        encryption_algorithm=serialization.NoEncryption()
    )

    # Serialize the public key to PEM format
    public_pem = public_key.public_bytes(
        encoding=serialization.Encoding.PEM,
        format=serialization.PublicFormat.SubjectPublicKeyInfo
    )

    # Save the keys to files
    with open(private_key_path, 'wb') as private_file:
        private_file.write(private_pem)

    with open(public_key_path, 'wb') as public_file:
        public_file.write(public_pem)

    # Print the keys
    print("Private Key (PEM format):")
    print(private_pem.decode())

    print("Public Key (PEM format):")
    print(public_pem.decode())

    print("Keys have been generated and saved.")

# Function to sign a file
def sign_file(private_key_path, file_path, signature_path):
    # Load the private key from PEM format
    with open(private_key_path, 'rb') as private_file:
        private_key = serialization.load_pem_private_key(
            private_file.read(),
```

```python
        password=None
    )
    
    # Read the file content
    with open(file_path, 'rb') as file:
        file_content = file.read()
    
    # Create a hash of the file content
    digest = hashes.Hash(hashes.SHA256())
    digest.update(file_content)
    hashed_message = digest.finalize()
    
    # Sign the hashed message
    signature = private_key.sign(
        hashed_message,
        hashes.SHA256()
    )
    
    # Save the signature to a file
    with open(signature_path, 'wb') as sig_file:
        sig_file.write(signature)
    
    # Print the signature
    print("Signature (Base64 encoded):")
    print(base64.b64encode(signature).decode())
    
    print("File has been signed and signature saved.")

# Function to verify a file's signature
def verify_file_signature(public_key_path, file_path, signature_path):
    # Load the public key from PEM format
    with open(public_key_path, 'rb') as public_file:
        public_key = serialization.load_pem_public_key(
            public_file.read()
        )
    
    # Read the file content
    with open(file_path, 'rb') as file:
        file_content = file.read()
    
    # Read the signature
    with open(signature_path, 'rb') as sig_file:
        signature = sig_file.read()
    
    # Print the signature read from file
    print("Signature read from file (Base64 encoded):")
    print(base64.b64encode(signature).decode())
    
    # Create a hash of the file content
    digest = hashes.Hash(hashes.SHA256())
    digest.update(file_content)
    hashed_message = digest.finalize()
    
    # Verify the signature
    try:
        public_key.verify(
            signature,
            hashed_message,
```

```python
            hashes.SHA256()
        )
        print("Signature is valid.")
    except InvalidSignature:
        print("Signature is invalid.")
    except Exception as e:
        print(f"An error occurred during verification: {e}")

# Main function to run the entire process
def main():
    # Define file paths
    private_key_path = 'private_key.pem'
    public_key_path = 'public_key.pem'
    file_path = 'example_file.txt'
    signature_path = 'signature.sig'

    # Generate and save keys
    generate_and_save_keys(private_key_path, public_key_path)

    # Check if the file exists
    if not os.path.exists(file_path):
        with open(file_path, 'wb') as file:
            file.write(b"This is a test file content.")
        print(f"File '{file_path}' created.")

    # Sign the file
    sign_file(private_key_path, file_path, signature_path)

    # Verify the file's signature
    verify_file_signature(public_key_path, file_path, signature_path)

if __name__ == "__main__":
    main()
```

Let's break down the code in detail, explaining each part thoroughly:

Imports

```
import os
import hashlib
import base64
from cryptography.hazmat.primitives.asymmetric import dsa
from cryptography.hazmat.primitives import hashes, serialization
from cryptography.exceptions import InvalidSignature
```

- import os: This module provides a way to use operating system-dependent functionality like reading or writing to the file system.
- import hashlib: This module includes hashing functions, but it is not used in this specific script. Instead, the cryptography.hazmat.primitives.hashes module is used.

- import base64: This module provides functions for encoding binary data to a text format (Base64), useful for printing or saving data in a readable format.
- from cryptography.hazmat.primitives.asymmetric import dsa: Imports the DSA (Digital Signature Algorithm) from the cryptography library, which is used for creating and verifying digital signatures.
- from cryptography.hazmat.primitives import hashes, serialization: Imports the hashes module for creating cryptographic hash functions and the serialization module for encoding/decoding keys.
- from cryptography.exceptions import InvalidSignature: Imports the InvalidSignature exception for handling errors related to signature verification.

Function to Generate and Save DSA Keys

```python
def generate_and_save_keys(private_key_path, public_key_path):
    # Generate a private key
    private_key = dsa.generate_private_key(key_size=2048)

    # Derive the public key
    public_key = private_key.public_key()

    # Serialize the private key to PEM format
    private_pem = private_key.private_bytes(
        encoding=serialization.Encoding.PEM,
        format=serialization.PrivateFormat.PKCS8,
        encryption_algorithm=serialization.NoEncryption()
    )

    # Serialize the public key to PEM format
    public_pem = public_key.public_bytes(
        encoding=serialization.Encoding.PEM,
        format=serialization.PublicFormat.SubjectPublicKeyInfo
    )

    # Save the keys to files
    with open(private_key_path, 'wb') as private_file:
        private_file.write(private_pem)

    with open(public_key_path, 'wb') as public_file:
        public_file.write(public_pem)

    # Print the keys
    print("Private Key (PEM format):")
    print(private_pem.decode())

    print("Public Key (PEM format):")
    print(public_pem.decode())

    print("Keys have been generated and saved.")
```

- generate_and_save_keys(private_key_path, public_key_path): Defines a function that generates DSA keys and saves them to specified file paths.
- private_key = dsa.generate_private_key(key_size=2048): Generates a private key with a key size of 2048 bits using the DSA algorithm. The key_size parameter defines the strength of the key.
- public_key = private_key.public_key(): Derives the corresponding public key from the generated private key.
- private_pem = private_key.private_bytes(...): Serializes the private key into PEM format. The private_bytes method takes several parameters:
  - encoding=serialization.Encoding.PEM: Specifies the encoding format as PEM.
  - format=serialization.PrivateFormat.PKCS8: Defines the private key format as PKCS8, a standard format for private keys.
  - encryption_algorithm=serialization.NoEncryption(): Indicates that the private key is not encrypted.
- public_pem = public_key.public_bytes(...): Serializes the public key into PEM format using similar parameters but for public keys:
  - format=serialization.PublicFormat.SubjectPublicKeyInfo: Standard format for public keys.
- with open(private_key_path, 'wb') as private_file:: Opens the file for writing the private key in binary mode.
- private_file.write(private_pem): Writes the serialized private key to the file.
- with open(public_key_path, 'wb') as public_file:: Opens the file for writing the public key in binary mode.
- public_file.write(public_pem): Writes the serialized public key to the file.
- print(private_pem.decode()): Decodes the PEM format private key from bytes to a string and prints it.
- print(public_pem.decode()): Similarly decodes and prints the PEM format public key.

Function to Sign a File

```
def sign_file(private_key_path, file_path, signature_path):
    # Load the private key from PEM format
    with open(private_key_path, 'rb') as private_file:
        private_key = serialization.load_pem_private_key(
            private_file.read(),
```

```
        password=None
    )

# Read the file content
with open(file_path, 'rb') as file:
    file_content = file.read()

# Create a hash of the file content
digest = hashes.Hash(hashes.SHA256())
digest.update(file_content)
hashed_message = digest.finalize()

# Sign the hashed message
signature = private_key.sign(
    hashed_message,
    hashes.SHA256()
)

# Save the signature to a file
with open(signature_path, 'wb') as sig_file:
    sig_file.write(signature)

# Print the signature
print("Signature (Base64 encoded):")
print(base64.b64encode(signature).decode())

print("File has been signed and signature saved.")
```

- sign_file(private_key_path, file_path, signature_path): Defines a function that signs a file and saves the signature.
- with open(private_key_path, 'rb') as private_file:: Opens the private key file in binary read mode.
- private_key = serialization.load_pem_private_key(...): Deserializes the private key from PEM format using load_pem_private_key. The password=None indicates that the key is not encrypted.
- with open(file_path, 'rb') as file:: Opens the file to be signed in binary read mode.
- file_content = file.read(): Reads the entire content of the file.
- digest = hashes.Hash(hashes.SHA256()): Creates a new hash object using SHA-256 for digest generation.
- digest.update(file_content): Updates the hash object with the file content.
- hashed_message = digest.finalize(): Finalizes the hash computation, producing the hash value.
- signature = private_key.sign(...): Signs the hashed message using the private key. The sign method takes the hashed message and the hash algorithm (SHA-256).
- with open(signature_path, 'wb') as sig_file:: Opens the file for writing the signature in binary mode.

- sig_file.write(signature): Writes the digital signature to the file.
- print(base64.b64encode(signature).decode()): Encodes the signature in Base64 format for readability and prints it.

Function to Verify a File's Signature

```
def verify_file_signature(public_key_path, file_path, signature_path):
    # Load the public key from PEM format
    with open(public_key_path, 'rb') as public_file:
        public_key = serialization.load_pem_public_key(
            public_file.read()
        )

    # Read the file content
    with open(file_path, 'rb') as file:
        file_content = file.read()

    # Read the signature
    with open(signature_path, 'rb') as sig_file:
        signature = sig_file.read()

    # Print the signature read from file
    print("Signature read from file (Base64 encoded):")
    print(base64.b64encode(signature).decode())

    # Create a hash of the file content
    digest = hashes.Hash(hashes.SHA256())
    digest.update(file_content)
    hashed_message = digest.finalize()

    # Verify the signature
    try:
        public_key.verify(
            signature,
            hashed_message,
            hashes.SHA256()
        )
        print("Signature is valid.")
    except InvalidSignature:
        print("Signature is invalid.")
    except Exception as e:
        print(f"An error occurred during verification: {e}")
```

- verify_file_signature(public_key_path, file_path, signature_path): Defines a function that verifies the authenticity of a file's signature.
- with open(public_key_path, 'rb') as public_file:: Opens the public key file in binary read mode.
- public_key = serialization.load_pem_public_key(...): Deserializes the public key from PEM format.

- with open(file_path, 'rb') as file:: Opens the file to be verified in binary read mode.
- file_content = file.read(): Reads the entire content of the file.
- with open(signature_path, 'rb') as sig_file:: Opens the signature file in binary read mode.
- signature = sig_file.read(): Reads the signature from the file.
- print(base64.b64encode(signature).decode()): Encodes the signature in Base64 format for readability and prints it.
- digest = hashes.Hash(hashes.SHA256()): Creates a hash object using SHA-256.
- digest.update(file_content): Updates the hash object with the file content.
- hashed_message = digest.finalize(): Finalizes the hash computation.
- public_key.verify(...): Verifies the signature using the public key, the hashed message, and SHA-256 as the hash algorithm. If the signature is invalid, an InvalidSignature exception is caught and a message is printed. Any other exceptions are also caught and printed.

Main Function

```
def main():
    # Define file paths
    private_key_path = 'private_key.pem'
    public_key_path = 'public_key.pem'
    file_path = 'example_file.txt'
    signature_path = 'signature.sig'

    # Generate and save keys
    generate_and_save_keys(private_key_path, public_key_path)

    # Check if the file exists
    if not os.path.exists(file_path):
        with open(file_path, 'wb') as file:
            file.write(b"This is a test file content.")
        print(f"File '{file_path}' created.")

    # Sign the file
    sign_file(private_key_path, file_path, signature_path)

    # Verify the file's signature
    verify_file_signature(public_key_path, file_path, signature_path)

if __name__ == "__main__":
    main()
```

- main(): The main function coordinates the workflow.
- private_key_path = 'private_key.pem': Sets the path for the private key file.

- public_key_path = 'public_key.pem': Sets the path for the public key file.
- file_path = 'example_file.txt': Sets the path for the file to be signed.
- signature_path = 'signature.sig': Sets the path for the signature file.
- generate_and_save_keys(private_key_path, public_key_path): Calls the function to generate and save DSA keys.
- if not os.path.exists(file_path):: Checks if the file exists. If not, creates it with sample content.
- sign_file(private_key_path, file_path, signature_path): Signs the file using the private key.
- verify_file_signature(public_key_path, file_path, signature_path): Verifies the file's signature using the public key.
- if __name__ == "__main__":: Ensures that the main() function is executed when the script is run directly.

Output

```
Private Key (PEM format):
-----BEGIN PRIVATE KEY-----
MIICZAIBADCCAjkGByqGSM44BAEwggIsAoIBAQCQJ9F/fb22ZohBoGHosigQsNfk
5oix8dAchoYgMxy6X4JufHMN9+eQ3lK9n2fTTf2XzXjPaThMzo8mriq2wXUUKSWz
8ecEpoqD+/IMsUdVtA/Z3uvS3Ae6D6XGgeWw0Yn6WgfofHiKUktqa1e4tnE0vB8N
Y5uLyVbNIZWx0RAYQW+WEK3vikLk1RECX3OPvqo2ZqdOXM8u5j4aD4nk6JTrfFdG
2H0V7pm72yx4k9tjHl2s7P81Sh4f/h6CG9meoCvxc5jBEcbaxZAAFh6DX0KEliQT
61iKz6VF67dVoalFqVIHkPiHiOi1wZRCC1wBknW4jVEApRLSA7r0qf34o6lXAiEA
pO9N0IensoSjoQhxX6Mp3CsO23FQrRsImUg9EN7uSSkCggEAQJJSw5oOn2Pq454A
yM2GMlp8tdlcNDJbFGIltxrn9mVmQtkMFsZTsfHPiiRST0yjCcSyzWzZDbklxevM
D6rwtUcgy3wiIhLKfBCntMWyYX0SNaEAop8h0orQu0YnzWCgtvmC2zUR8Xg8Y/FX
CwG+6R7VpuHxuTbd46fS5MW4p2VW4vLnH2lUD1v6GQngBuM2urycUs+oi0rJ5g4m
FR9wxInU3qSbnnYoQpez6963RjsivGInJIzLfnGNz50+tlZzHirfaldQ/qv31f5k
yJ5ij361dAXSgudulnpyK/qrSotT4/zyB1OnnJollYoDE2NMlu9F6k/gIwKd1DlX
gL2A2gQiAiBQf/duU5SPWsMQkEDAu7Vlk9onRo7z8Sh2+Kyjy9EkDQ==
-----END PRIVATE KEY-----

Public Key (PEM format):
-----BEGIN PUBLIC KEY-----
MIIDRjCCAjkGByqGSM44BAEwggIsAoIBAQCQJ9F/fb22ZohBoGHosigQsNfk5oix
8dAchoYgMxy6X4JufHMN9+eQ3lK9n2fTTf2XzXjPaThMzo8mriq2wXUUKSWz8ecE
poqD+/IMsUdVtA/Z3uvS3Ae6D6XGgeWw0Yn6WgfofHiKUktqa1e4tnE0vB8NY5uL
yVbNIZWx0RAYQW+WEK3vikLk1RECX3OPvqo2ZqdOXM8u5j4aD4nk6JTrfFdG2H0V
7pm72yx4k9tjHl2s7P81Sh4f/h6CG9meoCvxc5jBEcbaxZAAFh6DX0KEliQTG1iK
z6VF67dVoalFqVIHkPiHiOi1wZRCC1wBknW4jVEApRLSA7r0qf34o6lXAiEApO9N
0IensoSjoQhxX6Mp3CsO23FQrRsImUg9EN7uSSkCggEAQJJSw5oOn2Pq454AyM2G
Mlp8tdlcNDJbFGIltxrn9mVmQtkMFsZTsfHPiiRST0yjCcSyzWzZDbklxevMD6rw
tUcgy3wiIhLKfBCntMWyYX0SNaEAop8h0orQu0YnzWCgtvmC2zUR8Xg8Y/FXCwG+
6R7VpuHxuTbd46fS5MW4p2VW4vLnH2lUD1v6GQngBuM2urycUs+oi0rJ5g4mFR9w
xInU3qSbnnYoQpez6963RjsivGInJIzLfnGNz50+tlZzHirfaldQ/qv31f5kyJ5i
j361dAXSgudulnpyK/qrSotT4/zyB1OnnJollYoDE2NMlu9F6k/gIwKd1DlXgL2A
```

```
2gOCAQUAAoIBAAVJ9HtTGi8MAcwbcxS1cOMZHO2evXJiXI6IVbZzX2oW2PcTJ5sU
HP7T+lgvSpQ2Yh2AUTIKuFcvC8EPmLEjhjnueYRYcxeKRB9yRFAZqwBtNCCuz128
1/nIeVsB+levSDsm+g57JTrqJJCo7pt574m+nwc1oX3JKy9QlWgFyOcJPMCHvLcT
Czv00K3Uk5L/rzBWwUIVKwAu/z4b8AJD8olbYYbcf+KHFniA+9dq5TaRJPI0JQVu
sfiv5N0csSqcyOJRkI+vPltc9PG1d+gJ9hj54EQ7UvsbtrnvnDfsmsYMkFk8ok9v
+grQ0T57BK94wUL/GkLvxeAKlEj1nKatDig=
-----END PUBLIC KEY-----

Keys have been generated and saved.
Signature (Base64 encoded):
MEQCIDP8wVKGpJlHdIIHQd+tX7knVnvqTlmvLtlkKAnMut9VAiB5h15GJ8BJajoBXrwcYPItfF1iYQkgTPEaW
Y9dSwQBBg==
File has been signed and signature saved.
Signature read from file (Base64 encoded):
MEQCIDP8wVKGpJlHdIIHQd+tX7knVnvqTlmvLtlkKAnMut9VAiB5h15GJ8BJajoBXrwcYPItfF1iYQkgTPEaW
Y9dSwQBBg==
Signature is valid.
```

Project 6: GUI Tkinter for Signing and Verifying File

The purpose of this project is to develop a comprehensive application for performing cryptographic operations using Digital Signature Algorithm (DSA). This application, built with Tkinter for the graphical user interface, is designed to handle key generation, file signing, and signature verification. The primary goal is to provide a user-friendly interface for creating and managing DSA keys, signing files to ensure their authenticity, and verifying the signatures to validate the integrity of the files. By integrating these functionalities into a single application, users can efficiently manage and utilize cryptographic operations without needing to deal with low-level cryptographic details directly.

The application offers three main functionalities through its tabbed interface: generating and saving DSA keys, signing files, and verifying signatures. In the "Generate Keys" tab, users can create a new pair of private and public keys, which are then saved to specified files. The keys are serialized in PEM format, a widely used format for storing cryptographic keys and certificates. This functionality is crucial for users who need to generate key pairs for secure communications or data integrity purposes.

In the "Sign File" tab, users can sign files using their private key. The process involves hashing the file content, signing the hash with the private key, and saving the resulting signature to a file. This feature is essential for ensuring that files have not been tampered with and verifying the identity of the signer. The signature is encoded in Base64 for easy storage and transmission. The application also provides a straightforward method for users to browse and select files and paths, enhancing the usability of the signing process.

The "Verify Signature" tab allows users to validate the authenticity of signed files. Users can provide the public key, the file to be verified, and the signature file. The application will hash the file content, verify the signature using the public key, and display the result. This feature is vital for confirming the integrity and origin of files, ensuring that they are genuine and have not been altered. By providing a clear and organized interface for these cryptographic tasks, the application aims to simplify the process of maintaining data security and authenticity in various applications.

```python
import tkinter as tk
from tkinter import ttk, filedialog, messagebox
import os
import base64
from cryptography.hazmat.primitives.asymmetric import dsa
from cryptography.hazmat.primitives import hashes, serialization
from cryptography.exceptions import InvalidSignature

# Function to generate and save DSA keys
def generate_and_save_keys(private_key_path, public_key_path):
    try:
        # Generate a private key
        private_key = dsa.generate_private_key(key_size=2048)

        # Derive the public key
        public_key = private_key.public_key()

        # Serialize the private key to PEM format
        private_pem = private_key.private_bytes(
            encoding=serialization.Encoding.PEM,
            format=serialization.PrivateFormat.PKCS8,
            encryption_algorithm=serialization.NoEncryption()
        )

        # Serialize the public key to PEM format
        public_pem = public_key.public_bytes(
            encoding=serialization.Encoding.PEM,
            format=serialization.PublicFormat.SubjectPublicKeyInfo
        )

        # Save the keys to files
        with open(private_key_path, 'wb') as private_file:
            private_file.write(private_pem)

        with open(public_key_path, 'wb') as public_file:
            public_file.write(public_pem)

        # Return the keys as strings
        return private_pem.decode(), public_pem.decode()

    except Exception as e:
        messagebox.showerror("Error", f"An error occurred while generating keys: {e}")
        return None, None
```

```python
# Function to sign a file
def sign_file(private_key_path, file_path, signature_path):
    try:
        # Load the private key from PEM format
        with open(private_key_path, 'rb') as private_file:
            private_key = serialization.load_pem_private_key(
                private_file.read(),
                password=None
            )

        # Read the file content
        with open(file_path, 'rb') as file:
            file_content = file.read()

        # Create a hash of the file content
        digest = hashes.Hash(hashes.SHA256())
        digest.update(file_content)
        hashed_message = digest.finalize()

        # Sign the hashed message
        signature = private_key.sign(
            hashed_message,
            hashes.SHA256()
        )

        # Save the signature to a file
        with open(signature_path, 'wb') as sig_file:
            sig_file.write(signature)

        # Return the signature as Base64 encoded string
        return base64.b64encode(signature).decode()

    except Exception as e:
        messagebox.showerror("Error", f"An error occurred while signing the file: {e}")
        return None

# Function to verify a file's signature
def verify_file_signature(public_key_path, file_path, signature_path):
    try:
        # Load the public key from PEM format
        with open(public_key_path, 'rb') as public_file:
            public_key = serialization.load_pem_public_key(
                public_file.read()
            )

        # Read the file content
        with open(file_path, 'rb') as file:
            file_content = file.read()

        # Read the signature
        with open(signature_path, 'rb') as sig_file:
            signature = sig_file.read()

        # Create a hash of the file content
        digest = hashes.Hash(hashes.SHA256())
        digest.update(file_content)
        hashed_message = digest.finalize()
```

```python
        # Verify the signature
        public_key.verify(
            signature,
            hashed_message,
            hashes.SHA256()
        )
        return "Signature is valid."

    except InvalidSignature:
        return "Signature is invalid."

    except Exception as e:
        return f"An error occurred during verification: {e}"

# Create the Tkinter application
class CryptoApp(tk.Tk):
    def __init__(self):
        super().__init__()

        self.title("Cryptographic Operations")
        self.geometry("800x600")

        # Create tab control
        self.tab_control = ttk.Notebook(self)

        # Create tabs
        self.create_key_tab()
        self.create_sign_tab()
        self.create_verify_tab()

        # Add tabs to tab control
        self.tab_control.pack(expand=1, fill="both")

    def create_key_tab(self):
        self.key_tab = ttk.Frame(self.tab_control)
        self.tab_control.add(self.key_tab, text="Generate Keys")

        # Layout
        ttk.Label(self.key_tab, text="Generate and Save DSA Keys").grid(row=0, column=0, padx=10, pady=10)

        ttk.Label(self.key_tab, text="Private Key Path:").grid(row=1, column=0, padx=10, pady=5, sticky="w")
        self.private_key_entry = ttk.Entry(self.key_tab, width=60)
        self.private_key_entry.grid(row=1, column=1, padx=10, pady=5)
        ttk.Button(self.key_tab, text="Browse...", command=self.browse_private_key).grid(row=1, column=2, padx=10, pady=5)

        ttk.Label(self.key_tab, text="Public Key Path:").grid(row=2, column=0, padx=10, pady=5, sticky="w")
        self.public_key_entry = ttk.Entry(self.key_tab, width=60)
        self.public_key_entry.grid(row=2, column=1, padx=10, pady=5)
        ttk.Button(self.key_tab, text="Browse...", command=self.browse_public_key).grid(row=2, column=2, padx=10, pady=5)

        ttk.Button(self.key_tab, text="Generate Keys", command=self.generate_keys).grid(row=3, column=1, padx=10, pady=20)
```

```python
        self.key_output = tk.Text(self.key_tab, height=15, width=80)
        self.key_output.grid(row=4, column=0, columnspan=3, padx=10, pady=10)

    def create_sign_tab(self):
        self.sign_tab = ttk.Frame(self.tab_control)
        self.tab_control.add(self.sign_tab, text="Sign File")

        # Layout
        ttk.Label(self.sign_tab, text="Sign a File with DSA").grid(row=0, column=0, padx=10, pady=10)

        ttk.Label(self.sign_tab, text="Private Key Path:").grid(row=1, column=0, padx=10, pady=5, sticky="w")
        self.sign_private_key_entry = ttk.Entry(self.sign_tab, width=60)
        self.sign_private_key_entry.grid(row=1, column=1, padx=10, pady=5)
        ttk.Button(self.sign_tab, text="Browse...", command=self.browse_sign_private_key).grid(row=1, column=2, padx=10, pady=5)

        ttk.Label(self.sign_tab, text="File Path:").grid(row=2, column=0, padx=10, pady=5, sticky="w")
        self.sign_file_entry = ttk.Entry(self.sign_tab, width=60)
        self.sign_file_entry.grid(row=2, column=1, padx=10, pady=5)
        ttk.Button(self.sign_tab, text="Browse...", command=self.browse_sign_file).grid(row=2, column=2, padx=10, pady=5)

        ttk.Label(self.sign_tab, text="Signature Path:").grid(row=3, column=0, padx=10, pady=5, sticky="w")
        self.sign_signature_entry = ttk.Entry(self.sign_tab, width=60)
        self.sign_signature_entry.grid(row=3, column=1, padx=10, pady=5)
        ttk.Button(self.sign_tab, text="Browse...", command=self.browse_sign_signature).grid(row=3, column=2, padx=10, pady=5)

        ttk.Button(self.sign_tab, text="Sign File", command=self.sign_file).grid(row=4, column=1, padx=10, pady=20)

        self.sign_output = tk.Text(self.sign_tab, height=10, width=80)
        self.sign_output.grid(row=5, column=0, columnspan=3, padx=10, pady=10)

    def create_verify_tab(self):
        self.verify_tab = ttk.Frame(self.tab_control)
        self.tab_control.add(self.verify_tab, text="Verify Signature")

        # Layout
        ttk.Label(self.verify_tab, text="Verify a File's Signature").grid(row=0, column=0, padx=10, pady=10)

        ttk.Label(self.verify_tab, text="Public Key Path:").grid(row=1, column=0, padx=10, pady=5, sticky="w")
        self.verify_public_key_entry = ttk.Entry(self.verify_tab, width=60)
        self.verify_public_key_entry.grid(row=1, column=1, padx=10, pady=5)
        ttk.Button(self.verify_tab, text="Browse...", command=self.browse_verify_public_key).grid(row=1, column=2, padx=10, pady=5)

        ttk.Label(self.verify_tab, text="File Path:").grid(row=2, column=0, padx=10, pady=5, sticky="w")
        self.verify_file_entry = ttk.Entry(self.verify_tab, width=60)
        self.verify_file_entry.grid(row=2, column=1, padx=10, pady=5)
```

```python
        ttk.Button(self.verify_tab, text="Browse...",
command=self.browse_verify_file).grid(row=2, column=2, padx=10, pady=5)

        ttk.Label(self.verify_tab, text="Signature Path:").grid(row=3, column=0,
padx=10, pady=5, sticky="w")
        self.verify_signature_entry = ttk.Entry(self.verify_tab, width=60)
        self.verify_signature_entry.grid(row=3, column=1, padx=10, pady=5)
        ttk.Button(self.verify_tab, text="Browse...",
command=self.browse_verify_signature).grid(row=3, column=2, padx=10, pady=5)

        ttk.Button(self.verify_tab, text="Verify Signature",
command=self.verify_signature).grid(row=4, column=1, padx=10, pady=20)

        self.verify_output = tk.Text(self.verify_tab, height=10, width=80)
        self.verify_output.grid(row=5, column=0, columnspan=3, padx=10, pady=10)

    # Button command functions
    def browse_private_key(self):
        path = filedialog.asksaveasfilename(defaultextension=".pem", filetypes=[("PEM
Files", "*.pem")])
        if path:
            self.private_key_entry.delete(0, tk.END)
            self.private_key_entry.insert(0, path)

    def browse_public_key(self):
        path = filedialog.asksaveasfilename(defaultextension=".pem", filetypes=[("PEM
Files", "*.pem")])
        if path:
            self.public_key_entry.delete(0, tk.END)
            self.public_key_entry.insert(0, path)

    def browse_sign_private_key(self):
        path = filedialog.askopenfilename(filetypes=[("PEM Files", "*.pem")])
        if path:
            self.sign_private_key_entry.delete(0, tk.END)
            self.sign_private_key_entry.insert(0, path)

    def browse_sign_file(self):
        path = filedialog.askopenfilename()
        if path:
            self.sign_file_entry.delete(0, tk.END)
            self.sign_file_entry.insert(0, path)

    def browse_sign_signature(self):
        path = filedialog.asksaveasfilename(defaultextension=".sig",
filetypes=[("Signature Files", "*.sig")])
        if path:
            self.sign_signature_entry.delete(0, tk.END)
            self.sign_signature_entry.insert(0, path)

    def browse_verify_public_key(self):
        path = filedialog.askopenfilename(filetypes=[("PEM Files", "*.pem")])
        if path:
            self.verify_public_key_entry.delete(0, tk.END)
            self.verify_public_key_entry.insert(0, path)

    def browse_verify_file(self):
        path = filedialog.askopenfilename()
```

```
            if path:
                self.verify_file_entry.delete(0, tk.END)
                self.verify_file_entry.insert(0, path)

        def browse_verify_signature(self):
            path = filedialog.askopenfilename(filetypes=[("Signature Files", "*.sig")])
            if path:
                self.verify_signature_entry.delete(0, tk.END)
                self.verify_signature_entry.insert(0, path)

        def generate_keys(self):
            private_key_path = self.private_key_entry.get()
            public_key_path = self.public_key_entry.get()
            private_key_pem, public_key_pem = generate_and_save_keys(private_key_path, public_key_path)
            if private_key_pem and public_key_pem:
                self.key_output.delete(1.0, tk.END)
                self.key_output.insert(tk.END, "Private Key (PEM format):\n")
                self.key_output.insert(tk.END, private_key_pem + "\n")
                self.key_output.insert(tk.END, "Public Key (PEM format):\n")
                self.key_output.insert(tk.END, public_key_pem + "\n")

        def sign_file(self):
            private_key_path = self.sign_private_key_entry.get()
            file_path = self.sign_file_entry.get()
            signature_path = self.sign_signature_entry.get()
            signature = sign_file(private_key_path, file_path, signature_path)
            if signature:
                self.sign_output.delete(1.0, tk.END)
                self.sign_output.insert(tk.END, "Signature (Base64 encoded):\n")
                self.sign_output.insert(tk.END, signature + "\n")

        def verify_signature(self):
            public_key_path = self.verify_public_key_entry.get()
            file_path = self.verify_file_entry.get()
            signature_path = self.verify_signature_entry.get()
            result = verify_file_signature(public_key_path, file_path, signature_path)
            self.verify_output.delete(1.0, tk.END)
            self.verify_output.insert(tk.END, result + "\n")

if __name__ == "__main__":
    app = CryptoApp()
    app.mainloop()
```

Here's the explanation of each function:

1. generate_and_save_keys(private_key_path, public_key_path)

Purpose: This function generates a DSA key pair (private and public keys), serializes them into PEM format, and saves them to specified file paths.

```
def generate_and_save_keys(private_key_path, public_key_path):
    try:
        # Generate a private key
        private_key = dsa.generate_private_key(key_size=2048)
```

```
    # Derive the public key
    public_key = private_key.public_key()

    # Serialize the private key to PEM format
    private_pem = private_key.private_bytes(
        encoding=serialization.Encoding.PEM,
        format=serialization.PrivateFormat.PKCS8,
        encryption_algorithm=serialization.NoEncryption()
    )

    # Serialize the public key to PEM format
    public_pem = public_key.public_bytes(
        encoding=serialization.Encoding.PEM,
        format=serialization.PublicFormat.SubjectPublicKeyInfo
    )

    # Save the keys to files
    with open(private_key_path, 'wb') as private_file:
        private_file.write(private_pem)

    with open(public_key_path, 'wb') as public_file:
        public_file.write(public_pem)

    # Return the keys as strings
    return private_pem.decode(), public_pem.decode()

except Exception as e:
    messagebox.showerror("Error", f"An error occurred while generating keys: {e}")
    return None, None
```

- private_key = dsa.generate_private_key(key_size=2048): Generates a new private DSA key with a key size of 2048 bits.
- public_key = private_key.public_key(): Derives the corresponding public key from the private key.
- private_pem = private_key.private_bytes(...): Serializes the private key to PEM format using PKCS8 format without encryption.
- public_pem = public_key.public_bytes(...): Serializes the public key to PEM format using SubjectPublicKeyInfo format.
- with open(private_key_path, 'wb') as private_file:: Opens the file for the private key in binary write mode and saves the serialized private key.
- with open(public_key_path, 'wb') as public_file:: Opens the file for the public key in binary write mode and saves the serialized public key.
- return private_pem.decode(), public_pem.decode(): Returns the serialized keys as UTF-8 strings.

- messagebox.showerror("Error", f"An error occurred while generating keys: {e}"): Displays an error message if an exception occurs.

2. sign_file(private_key_path, file_path, signature_path)

Purpose: This function signs the content of a file using a private key and saves the resulting signature to a specified file path.

```
def sign_file(private_key_path, file_path, signature_path):
    try:
        # Load the private key from PEM format
        with open(private_key_path, 'rb') as private_file:
            private_key = serialization.load_pem_private_key(
                private_file.read(),
                password=None
            )

        # Read the file content
        with open(file_path, 'rb') as file:
            file_content = file.read()

        # Create a hash of the file content
        digest = hashes.Hash(hashes.SHA256())
        digest.update(file_content)
        hashed_message = digest.finalize()

        # Sign the hashed message
        signature = private_key.sign(
            hashed_message,
            hashes.SHA256()
        )

        # Save the signature to a file
        with open(signature_path, 'wb') as sig_file:
            sig_file.write(signature)

        # Return the signature as Base64 encoded string
        return base64.b64encode(signature).decode()

    except Exception as e:
        messagebox.showerror("Error", f"An error occurred while signing the file: {e}")
        return None
```

- with open(private_key_path, 'rb') as private_file:: Opens the private key file in binary read mode.
- private_key = serialization.load_pem_private_key(...): Loads the private key from PEM format.
- with open(file_path, 'rb') as file:: Opens the file to be signed in binary read mode.

- digest = hashes.Hash(hashes.SHA256()): Creates a SHA-256 hash object.
- digest.update(file_content): Updates the hash object with the file content.
- hashed_message = digest.finalize(): Finalizes the hash computation to get the digest.
- signature = private_key.sign(...): Signs the hashed message using the private key and SHA-256.
- with open(signature_path, 'wb') as sig_file:: Opens the file to save the signature in binary write mode.
- return base64.b64encode(signature).decode(): Returns the signature encoded in Base64 format.
- messagebox.showerror("Error", f"An error occurred while signing the file: {e}"): Displays an error message if an exception occurs.

3. verify_file_signature(public_key_path, file_path, signature_path)

Purpose: This function verifies the signature of a file using a public key and returns the result of the verification.

```
def verify_file_signature(public_key_path, file_path, signature_path):
    try:
        # Load the public key from PEM format
        with open(public_key_path, 'rb') as public_file:
            public_key = serialization.load_pem_public_key(
                public_file.read()
            )

        # Read the file content
        with open(file_path, 'rb') as file:
            file_content = file.read()

        # Read the signature
        with open(signature_path, 'rb') as sig_file:
            signature = sig_file.read()

        # Create a hash of the file content
        digest = hashes.Hash(hashes.SHA256())
        digest.update(file_content)
        hashed_message = digest.finalize()

        # Verify the signature
        public_key.verify(
            signature,
            hashed_message,
            hashes.SHA256()
        )
        return "Signature is valid."
```

```
except InvalidSignature:
    return "Signature is invalid."

except Exception as e:
    return f"An error occurred during verification: {e}"
```

- with open(public_key_path, 'rb') as public_file:: Opens the public key file in binary read mode.
- public_key = serialization.load_pem_public_key(...): Loads the public key from PEM format.
- with open(file_path, 'rb') as file:: Opens the file to verify in binary read mode.
- with open(signature_path, 'rb') as sig_file:: Opens the file containing the signature in binary read mode.
- digest = hashes.Hash(hashes.SHA256()): Creates a SHA-256 hash object.
- digest.update(file_content): Updates the hash object with the file content.
- hashed_message = digest.finalize(): Finalizes the hash computation to get the digest.
- public_key.verify(...): Verifies the signature against the hashed message using the public key and SHA-256.
- return "Signature is valid.": Returns a message indicating the signature is valid if no exception occurs.
- return "Signature is invalid.": Returns a message indicating the signature is invalid if InvalidSignature exception is raised.
- return f"An error occurred during verification: {e}": Returns an error message if an exception occurs during verification.

Here's the explanation of each function in the CryptoApp class:

__init__ Method

```
def __init__(self):
    super().__init__()

    self.title("Cryptographic Operations")
    self.geometry("800x600")

    # Create tab control
    self.tab_control = ttk.Notebook(self)

    # Create tabs
    self.create_key_tab()
```

```
    self.create_sign_tab()
    self.create_verify_tab()

    # Add tabs to tab control
    self.tab_control.pack(expand=1, fill="both")
```

- Purpose: Initializes the main window of the Tkinter application.
- super().__init__(): Calls the initializer of the parent tk.Tk class to set up the window.
- self.title("Cryptographic Operations"): Sets the title of the application window.
- self.geometry("800x600"): Specifies the size of the window (800x600 pixels).
- self.tab_control = ttk.Notebook(self): Creates a tab control (notebook) widget to hold multiple tabs.
- self.create_key_tab(): Calls a method to create the "Generate Keys" tab.
- self.create_sign_tab(): Calls a method to create the "Sign File" tab.
- self.create_verify_tab(): Calls a method to create the "Verify Signature" tab.
- self.tab_control.pack(expand=1, fill="both"): Packs the tab control into the window, allowing it to expand and fill the window.

create_key_tab Method

```
def create_key_tab(self):
    self.key_tab = ttk.Frame(self.tab_control)
    self.tab_control.add(self.key_tab, text="Generate Keys")

    # Layout
    ttk.Label(self.key_tab, text="Generate and Save DSA Keys").grid(row=0, column=0, padx=10, pady=10)

    ttk.Label(self.key_tab, text="Private Key Path:").grid(row=1, column=0, padx=10, pady=5, sticky="w")
    self.private_key_entry = ttk.Entry(self.key_tab, width=60)
    self.private_key_entry.grid(row=1, column=1, padx=10, pady=5)
    ttk.Button(self.key_tab, text="Browse...", command=self.browse_private_key).grid(row=1, column=2, padx=10, pady=5)

    ttk.Label(self.key_tab, text="Public Key Path:").grid(row=2, column=0, padx=10, pady=5, sticky="w")
    self.public_key_entry = ttk.Entry(self.key_tab, width=60)
    self.public_key_entry.grid(row=2, column=1, padx=10, pady=5)
    ttk.Button(self.key_tab, text="Browse...", command=self.browse_public_key).grid(row=2, column=2, padx=10, pady=5)

    ttk.Button(self.key_tab, text="Generate Keys", command=self.generate_keys).grid(row=3, column=1, padx=10, pady=20)

    self.key_output = tk.Text(self.key_tab, height=15, width=80)
```

```
self.key_output.grid(row=4, column=0, columnspan=3, padx=10, pady=10)
```

- Purpose: Sets up the "Generate Keys" tab.
- self.key_tab = ttk.Frame(self.tab_control): Creates a new frame for the "Generate Keys" tab.
- self.tab_control.add(self.key_tab, text="Generate Keys"): Adds the frame as a tab labeled "Generate Keys" to the tab control.
- ttk.Label(self.key_tab, text="Generate and Save DSA Keys"): Adds a label to the tab.
- ttk.Label(self.key_tab, text="Private Key Path:"): Adds a label for the private key path input.
- self.private_key_entry = ttk.Entry(self.key_tab, width=60): Adds an entry widget for the private key path.
- ttk.Button(self.key_tab, text="Browse...", command=self.browse_private_key): Adds a button to open a file dialog for selecting the private key file.
- ttk.Label(self.key_tab, text="Public Key Path:"): Adds a label for the public key path input.
- self.public_key_entry = ttk.Entry(self.key_tab, width=60): Adds an entry widget for the public key path.
- ttk.Button(self.key_tab, text="Browse...", command=self.browse_public_key): Adds a button to open a file dialog for selecting the public key file.
- ttk.Button(self.key_tab, text="Generate Keys", command=self.generate_keys): Adds a button to trigger the key generation process.
- self.key_output = tk.Text(self.key_tab, height=15, width=80): Adds a text widget to display the generated keys or any relevant output.

create_sign_tab Method

```
def create_sign_tab(self):
    self.sign_tab = ttk.Frame(self.tab_control)
    self.tab_control.add(self.sign_tab, text="Sign File")

    # Layout
    ttk.Label(self.sign_tab, text="Sign a File with DSA").grid(row=0, column=0, padx=10, pady=10)

    ttk.Label(self.sign_tab, text="Private Key Path:").grid(row=1, column=0, padx=10, pady=5, sticky="w")
    self.sign_private_key_entry = ttk.Entry(self.sign_tab, width=60)
    self.sign_private_key_entry.grid(row=1, column=1, padx=10, pady=5)
```

```
    ttk.Button(self.sign_tab, text="Browse...",
command=self.browse_sign_private_key).grid(row=1, column=2, padx=10, pady=5)

    ttk.Label(self.sign_tab, text="File Path:").grid(row=2, column=0, padx=10,
pady=5, sticky="w")
    self.sign_file_entry = ttk.Entry(self.sign_tab, width=60)
    self.sign_file_entry.grid(row=2, column=1, padx=10, pady=5)
    ttk.Button(self.sign_tab, text="Browse...",
command=self.browse_sign_file).grid(row=2, column=2, padx=10, pady=5)

    ttk.Label(self.sign_tab, text="Signature Path:").grid(row=3, column=0, padx=10,
pady=5, sticky="w")
    self.sign_signature_entry = ttk.Entry(self.sign_tab, width=60)
    self.sign_signature_entry.grid(row=3, column=1, padx=10, pady=5)
    ttk.Button(self.sign_tab, text="Browse...",
command=self.browse_sign_signature).grid(row=3, column=2, padx=10, pady=5)

    ttk.Button(self.sign_tab, text="Sign File", command=self.sign_file).grid(row=4,
column=1, padx=10, pady=20)

    self.sign_output = tk.Text(self.sign_tab, height=10, width=80)
    self.sign_output.grid(row=5, column=0, columnspan=3, padx=10, pady=10)
```

- Purpose: Sets up the "Sign File" tab.
- self.sign_tab = ttk.Frame(self.tab_control): Creates a new frame for the "Sign File" tab.
- self.tab_control.add(self.sign_tab, text="Sign File"): Adds the frame as a tab labeled "Sign File" to the tab control.
- ttk.Label(self.sign_tab, text="Sign a File with DSA"): Adds a label to the tab.
- ttk.Label(self.sign_tab, text="Private Key Path:"): Adds a label for the private key path input.
- self.sign_private_key_entry = ttk.Entry(self.sign_tab, width=60): Adds an entry widget for the private key path.
- ttk.Button(self.sign_tab, text="Browse...", command=self.browse_sign_private_key): Adds a button to open a file dialog for selecting the private key file.
- ttk.Label(self.sign_tab, text="File Path:"): Adds a label for the file to be signed.
- self.sign_file_entry = ttk.Entry(self.sign_tab, width=60): Adds an entry widget for the file path.
- ttk.Button(self.sign_tab, text="Browse...", command=self.browse_sign_file): Adds a button to open a file dialog for selecting the file to be signed.
- ttk.Label(self.sign_tab, text="Signature Path:"): Adds a label for the signature output path.

- self.sign_signature_entry = ttk.Entry(self.sign_tab, width=60): Adds an entry widget for the signature file path.
- ttk.Button(self.sign_tab, text="Browse...", command=self.browse_sign_signature): Adds a button to open a file dialog for selecting the signature file path.
- ttk.Button(self.sign_tab, text="Sign File", command=self.sign_file): Adds a button to trigger the file signing process.
- self.sign_output = tk.Text(self.sign_tab, height=10, width=80): Adds a text widget to display the result of the signing operation.

create_verify_tab Method

```
def create_verify_tab(self):
    self.verify_tab = ttk.Frame(self.tab_control)
    self.tab_control.add(self.verify_tab, text="Verify Signature")

    # Layout
    ttk.Label(self.verify_tab, text="Verify a File's Signature").grid(row=0,
column=0, padx=10, pady=10)

    ttk.Label(self.verify_tab, text="Public Key Path:").grid(row=1, column=0,
padx=10, pady=5, sticky="w")
    self.verify_public_key_entry = ttk.Entry(self.verify_tab, width=60)
    self.verify_public_key_entry.grid(row=1, column=1, padx=10, pady=5)
    ttk.Button(self.verify_tab, text="Browse...",
command=self.browse_verify_public_key).grid(row=1, column=2, padx=10, pady=5)

    ttk.Label(self.verify_tab, text="File Path:").grid(row=2, column=0, padx=10,
pady=5, sticky="w")
    self.verify_file_entry = ttk.Entry(self.verify_tab, width=60)
    self.verify_file_entry.grid(row=2, column=1, padx=10, pady=5)
    ttk.Button(self.verify_tab, text="Browse...",
command=self.browse_verify_file).grid(row=2, column=2, padx=10, pady=5)

    ttk.Label(self.verify_tab, text="Signature Path:").grid(row=3, column=0, padx=10,
pady=5, sticky="w")
    self.verify_signature_entry = ttk.Entry(self.verify_tab, width=60)
    self.verify_signature_entry.grid(row=3, column=1, padx=10, pady=5)
    ttk.Button(self.verify_tab, text="Browse...",
command=self.browse_verify_signature).grid(row=3, column=2, padx=10, pady=5)

    ttk.Button(self.verify_tab, text="Verify Signature",
command=self.verify_signature).grid(row=4, column=1, padx=10, pady=20)

    self.verify_output = tk.Text(self.verify_tab, height=10, width=80)
    self.verify_output.grid(row=5, column=0, columnspan=3, padx=10, pady=10)
```

- Purpose: Sets up the "Verify Signature" tab.

- self.verify_tab = ttk.Frame(self.tab_control): Creates a new frame for the "Verify Signature" tab.
- self.tab_control.add(self.verify_tab, text="Verify Signature"): Adds the frame as a tab labeled "Verify Signature" to the tab control.
- ttk.Label(self.verify_tab, text="Verify a File's Signature"): Adds a label to the tab.
- ttk.Label(self.verify_tab, text="Public Key Path:"): Adds a label for the public key path input.
- self.verify_public_key_entry = ttk.Entry(self.verify_tab, width=60): Adds an entry widget for the public key path.
- ttk.Button(self.verify_tab, text="Browse...", command=self.browse_verify_public_key): Adds a button to open a file dialog for selecting the public key file.
- ttk.Label(self.verify_tab, text="File Path:"): Adds a label for the file to be verified.
- self.verify_file_entry = ttk.Entry(self.verify_tab, width=60): Adds an entry widget for the file path.
- ttk.Button(self.verify_tab, text="Browse...", command=self.browse_verify_file): Adds a button to open a file dialog for selecting the file to be verified.
- ttk.Label(self.verify_tab, text="Signature Path:"): Adds a label for the signature file path.
- self.verify_signature_entry = ttk.Entry(self.verify_tab, width=60): Adds an entry widget for the signature file path.
- ttk.Button(self.verify_tab, text="Browse...", command=self.browse_verify_signature): Adds a button to open a file dialog for selecting the signature file path.
- ttk.Button(self.verify_tab, text="Verify Signature", command=self.verify_signature): Adds a button to trigger the signature verification process.
- self.verify_output = tk.Text(self.verify_tab, height=10, width=80): Adds a text widget to display the result of the signature verification.

These methods together create a comprehensive GUI application for cryptographic operations, including generating keys, signing files, and verifying signatures. Each tab provides a specific functionality and allows users to interact with file paths and cryptographic keys through intuitive widgets.

Here's the explanation of the other functions:

browse_private_key

```
def browse_private_key(self):
    path = filedialog.asksaveasfilename(defaultextension=".pem", filetypes=[("PEM 
Files", "*.pem")])
    if path:
        self.private_key_entry.delete(0, tk.END)
        self.private_key_entry.insert(0, path)
```

- Purpose: Opens a file dialog for the user to choose a location and name for saving the private key file.
- filedialog.asksaveasfilename(): Opens a file dialog that allows the user to specify a file path to save a file. It defaults to .pem file extension and filters the file types to show only PEM files.
- if path:: Checks if the user selected a file path (i.e., did not cancel the dialog).
- self.private_key_entry.delete(0, tk.END): Clears the current text in the private_key_entry widget.
- self.private_key_entry.insert(0, path): Inserts the selected file path into the private_key_entry widget.

browse_public_key

```
def browse_public_key(self):
    path = filedialog.asksaveasfilename(defaultextension=".pem", filetypes=[("PEM 
Files", "*.pem")])
    if path:
        self.public_key_entry.delete(0, tk.END)
        self.public_key_entry.insert(0, path)
```

- Purpose: Similar to browse_private_key, but for selecting a file path to save the public key.
- filedialog.asksaveasfilename(): Opens a file dialog to choose a location and name for the public key file, with a .pem extension by default.
- if path:: Ensures that a file path was selected.
- self.public_key_entry.delete(0, tk.END): Clears the current text in the public_key_entry widget.
- self.public_key_entry.insert(0, path): Inserts the selected file path into the public_key_entry widget.

browse_sign_private_key

```
def browse_sign_private_key(self):
    path = filedialog.askopenfilename(filetypes=[("PEM Files", "*.pem")])
    if path:
        self.sign_private_key_entry.delete(0, tk.END)
        self.sign_private_key_entry.insert(0, path)
```

- Purpose: Opens a file dialog for the user to select a private key file for signing.
- filedialog.askopenfilename(): Opens a file dialog that allows the user to select an existing file. It filters the files to show only PEM files.
- if path:: Checks if a file was selected.
- self.sign_private_key_entry.delete(0, tk.END): Clears the current text in the sign_private_key_entry widget.
- self.sign_private_key_entry.insert(0, path): Inserts the selected file path into the sign_private_key_entry widget.

browse_sign_file

```
def browse_sign_file(self):
    path = filedialog.askopenfilename()
    if path:
        self.sign_file_entry.delete(0, tk.END)
        self.sign_file_entry.insert(0, path)
```

- Purpose: Opens a file dialog for the user to select a file to be signed.
- filedialog.askopenfilename(): Opens a file dialog to select an existing file without filtering by type.
- if path:: Ensures a file was selected.
- self.sign_file_entry.delete(0, tk.END): Clears the current text in the sign_file_entry widget.
- self.sign_file_entry.insert(0, path): Inserts the selected file path into the sign_file_entry widget.

browse_sign_signature

```
def browse_sign_signature(self):
    path = filedialog.asksaveasfilename(defaultextension=".sig",
filetypes=[("Signature Files", "*.sig")])
    if path:
```

```
        self.sign_signature_entry.delete(0, tk.END)
        self.sign_signature_entry.insert(0, path)
```

- Purpose: Opens a file dialog for the user to specify a file path to save the signature.
- filedialog.asksaveasfilename(): Opens a file dialog to choose a location and name for the signature file, with a .sig extension by default.
- if path:: Checks if a path was selected.
- self.sign_signature_entry.delete(0, tk.END): Clears the current text in the sign_signature_entry widget.
- self.sign_signature_entry.insert(0, path): Inserts the selected file path into the sign_signature_entry widget.

browse_verify_public_key

```
def browse_verify_public_key(self):
    path = filedialog.askopenfilename(filetypes=[("PEM Files", "*.pem")])
    if path:
        self.verify_public_key_entry.delete(0, tk.END)
        self.verify_public_key_entry.insert(0, path)
```

- Purpose: Opens a file dialog for the user to select a public key file for verification.
- filedialog.askopenfilename(): Opens a file dialog to select an existing file, filtered to show only PEM files.
- if path:: Checks if a file was selected.
- self.verify_public_key_entry.delete(0, tk.END): Clears the current text in the verify_public_key_entry widget.
- self.verify_public_key_entry.insert(0, path): Inserts the selected file path into the verify_public_key_entry widget.

browse_verify_file

```
def browse_verify_file(self):
    path = filedialog.askopenfilename()
    if path:
        self.verify_file_entry.delete(0, tk.END)
        self.verify_file_entry.insert(0, path)
```

- Purpose: Opens a file dialog for the user to select the file to be verified.

- filedialog.askopenfilename(): Opens a file dialog to select an existing file without filtering by type.
- if path:: Ensures a file was selected.
- self.verify_file_entry.delete(0, tk.END): Clears the current text in the verify_file_entry widget.
- self.verify_file_entry.insert(0, path): Inserts the selected file path into the verify_file_entry widget.

browse_verify_signature

```
def browse_verify_signature(self):
    path = filedialog.askopenfilename(filetypes=[("Signature Files", "*.sig")])
    if path:
        self.verify_signature_entry.delete(0, tk.END)
        self.verify_signature_entry.insert(0, path)
```

- Purpose: Opens a file dialog for the user to select the signature file for verification.
- filedialog.askopenfilename(): Opens a file dialog to select an existing file, filtered to show only signature files.
- if path:: Checks if a file was selected.
- self.verify_signature_entry.delete(0, tk.END): Clears the current text in the verify_signature_entry widget.
- self.verify_signature_entry.insert(0, path): Inserts the selected file path into the verify_signature_entry widget.

generate_keys

```
def generate_keys(self):
    private_key_path = self.private_key_entry.get()
    public_key_path = self.public_key_entry.get()
    private_key_pem, public_key_pem = generate_and_save_keys(private_key_path, public_key_path)
    if private_key_pem and public_key_pem:
        self.key_output.delete(1.0, tk.END)
        self.key_output.insert(tk.END, "Private Key (PEM format):\n")
        self.key_output.insert(tk.END, private_key_pem + "\n")
        self.key_output.insert(tk.END, "Public Key (PEM format):\n")
        self.key_output.insert(tk.END, public_key_pem + "\n")
```

- Purpose: Generates and saves DSA keys and displays them in the text widget.

- private_key_path = self.private_key_entry.get(): Retrieves the file path for the private key from the private_key_entry widget.
- public_key_path = self.public_key_entry.get(): Retrieves the file path for the public key from the public_key_entry widget.
- private_key_pem, public_key_pem = generate_and_save_keys(private_key_path, public_key_path): Calls a function to generate and save the keys and returns them in PEM format.
- if private_key_pem and public_key_pem:: Checks if keys were successfully generated.
- self.key_output.delete(1.0, tk.END): Clears the current text in the key_output widget.
- self.key_output.insert(tk.END, "Private Key (PEM format):\n"): Inserts the label for the private key.
- self.key_output.insert(tk.END, private_key_pem + "\n"): Inserts the private key in PEM format.
- self.key_output.insert(tk.END, "Public Key (PEM format):\n"): Inserts the label for the public key.
- self.key_output.insert(tk.END, public_key_pem + "\n"): Inserts the public key in PEM format.

sign_file

```
def sign_file(self):
    private_key_path = self.sign_private_key_entry.get()
    file_path = self.sign_file_entry.get()
    signature_path = self.sign_signature_entry.get()
    signature = sign_file(private_key_path, file_path, signature_path)
    if signature:
        self.sign_output.delete(1.0, tk.END)
        self.sign_output.insert(tk.END, "Signature (Base64 encoded):\n")
        self.sign_output.insert(tk.END, signature + "\n")
```

- Purpose: Signs a file and displays the signature in the text widget.
- private_key_path = self.sign_private_key_entry.get(): Retrieves the private key file path from the sign_private_key_entry widget.
- file_path = self.sign_file_entry.get(): Retrieves the file path to be signed from the sign_file_entry widget.
- signature_path = self.sign_signature_entry.get(): Retrieves the file path to save the signature from the sign_signature_entry widget.

- signature = sign_file(private_key_path, file_path, signature_path): Calls a function to sign the file and returns the signature in Base64 format.
- if signature:: Checks if a signature was successfully generated.
- self.sign_output.delete(1.0, tk.END): Clears the current text in the sign_output widget.
- self.sign_output.insert(tk.END, "Signature (Base64 encoded):\n"): Inserts the label for the signature.
- self.sign_output.insert(tk.END, signature + "\n"): Inserts the Base64-encoded signature.

verify_signature

```
def verify_signature(self):
    public_key_path = self.verify_public_key_entry.get()
    file_path = self.verify_file_entry.get()
    signature_path = self.verify_signature_entry.get()
    result = verify_file_signature(public_key_path, file_path, signature_path)
    self.verify_output.delete(1.0, tk.END)
    self.verify_output.insert(tk.END, result + "\n")
```

- Purpose: Verifies a file's signature and displays the result.
- public_key_path = self.verify_public_key_entry.get(): Retrieves the public key file path from the verify_public_key_entry widget.
- file_path = self.verify_file_entry.get(): Retrieves the file path to be verified from the verify_file_entry widget.
- signature_path = self.verify_signature_entry.get(): Retrieves the signature file path from the verify_signature_entry widget.
- result = verify_file_signature(public_key_path, file_path, signature_path): Calls a function to verify the signature and returns the result.
- self.verify_output.delete(1.0, tk.END): Clears the current text in the verify_output widget.
- self.verify_output.insert(tk.END, result + "\n"): Inserts the verification result into the verify_output widget.

Each function handles user interactions with the GUI, allowing file and key selection, and performs the necessary cryptographic operations using the selected files and keys.

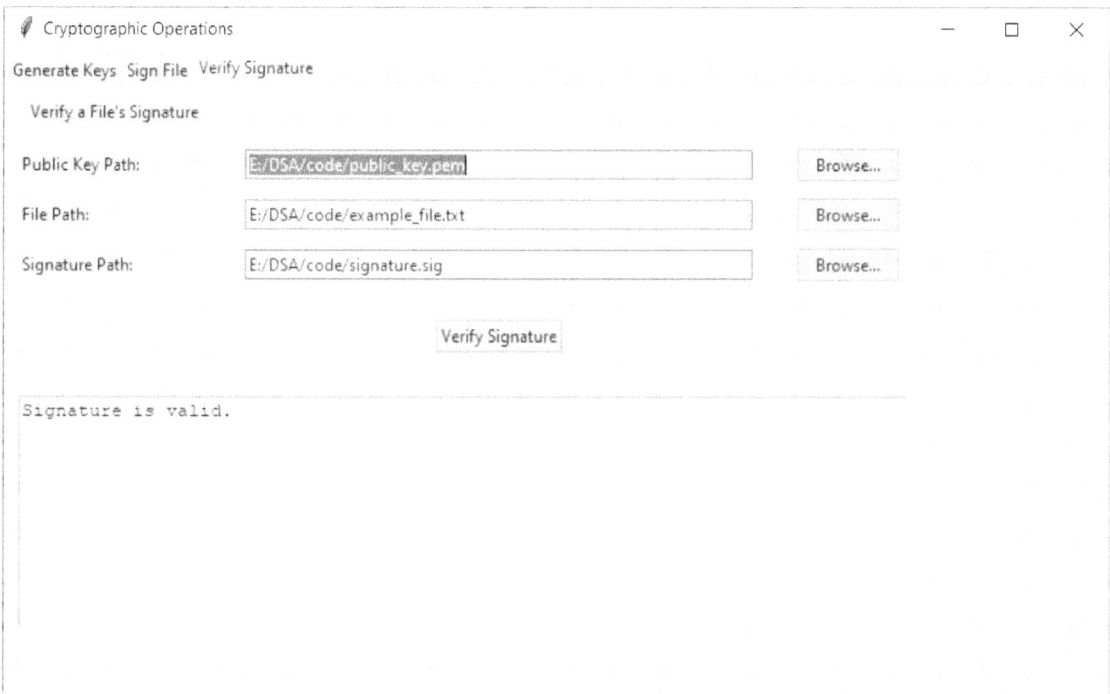

Project 7: Managing Data Integrity and Security on Synthetic Financial Dataset

This project focuses on creating and managing synthetic financial datasets with an emphasis on data integrity and security. It combines data generation, digital signing, and signature verification to ensure the authenticity and integrity of financial records. The core objectives include generating realistic financial data, securing it with digital signatures, and verifying those signatures to detect any tampering or corruption.

The first phase of the project involves generating a synthetic financial dataset with multiple columns, including transaction IDs, account numbers, amounts, currencies, timestamps, and transaction types. This data serves as a representative sample for testing and validation purposes. By using random values and timestamps, the dataset mimics real-world financial transactions, providing a diverse range of data for further processing.

The second phase centers on the generation and management of DSA (Digital Signature Algorithm) keys. This step includes creating both private and public keys used for signing and verifying the dataset. The private key is kept secret and used to create digital signatures, while the public key is distributed to verify the signatures. This ensures that the dataset's integrity can be validated by anyone with access to the public key, making it a critical component of the security process.

Finally, the project implements the signing and verification of the dataset. Each entry in the dataset is signed using the private key, and these signatures are saved separately. Verification involves checking each signature against the corresponding entry in the dataset using the public key. This process helps detect any unauthorized changes to the data, ensuring that the dataset remains trustworthy and accurate throughout its lifecycle. By combining these steps, the project demonstrates a practical approach to secure data handling and verification in financial applications.

```python
import pandas as pd
import numpy as np
from Crypto.PublicKey import DSA
from Crypto.Signature import DSS
from Crypto.Hash import SHA256
import datetime
import os

def generate_financial_data(num_entries=100):
    """Generate a synthetic financial dataset with multiple columns."""
    np.random.seed(0)  # For reproducibility
    
    data = {
        'transaction_id': np.arange(1, num_entries + 1),
        'account_number': [f'ACCT{np.random.randint(100000, 999999)}' for _ in range(num_entries)],
        'amount': np.random.uniform(1, 10000, num_entries),
        'currency': np.random.choice(['USD', 'EUR', 'GBP'], num_entries),
        'timestamp': [datetime.datetime.now() - datetime.timedelta(days=np.random.randint(1, 365)) for _ in range(num_entries)],
        'transaction_type': np.random.choice(['credit', 'debit'], num_entries)
    }
    
    df = pd.DataFrame(data)
    return df

def save_dataset(df, file_path):
    """Save the DataFrame to a CSV file."""
    df.to_csv(file_path, index=False)
    print(f"Dataset saved to {file_path}")

def generate_dsa_keys(private_key_path, public_key_path, key_size=2048):
    """Generate DSA keys and save to files."""
    try:
        key = DSA.generate(key_size)
        private_key = key.export_key(format='PEM')
        public_key = key.publickey().export_key(format='PEM')
        
        with open(private_key_path, 'wb') as priv_file:
            priv_file.write(private_key)
```

```python
            with open(public_key_path, 'wb') as pub_file:
                pub_file.write(public_key)

            print(f"Keys generated and saved to {private_key_path} and {public_key_path}")

        except Exception as e:
            print(f"Error generating keys: {e}")

    def sign_dataset(private_key_path, data_file_path, signature_file_path):
        """Sign each entry in the dataset and save the signatures."""
        try:
            with open(private_key_path, 'rb') as key_file:
                private_key = DSA.import_key(key_file.read())

            df = pd.read_csv(data_file_path)
            signatures = []

            for index, row in df.iterrows():
                data = row.to_dict()
                data_str = str(data).encode()
                data_hash = SHA256.new(data_str)
                signer = DSS.new(private_key, 'fips-186-3')
                signature = signer.sign(data_hash)
                signatures.append(signature)

            # Save signatures
            np.save(signature_file_path, signatures)
            print(f"Signatures saved to {signature_file_path}")

        except Exception as e:
            print(f"Error signing dataset: {e}")

    def verify_dataset_signatures(public_key_path, data_file_path, signature_file_path):
        """Verify the signatures of each entry in the dataset."""
        try:
            with open(public_key_path, 'rb') as key_file:
                public_key = DSA.import_key(key_file.read())

            df = pd.read_csv(data_file_path)
            signatures = np.load(signature_file_path)

            verifier = DSS.new(public_key, 'fips-186-3')
            for index, row in df.iterrows():
                data = row.to_dict()
                data_str = str(data).encode()
                data_hash = SHA256.new(data_str)
                signature = signatures[index]

                try:
                    verifier.verify(data_hash, signature)
                    print(f"Signature for entry {index + 1} is valid.")
                except (ValueError, TypeError):
                    print(f"Signature for entry {index + 1} is invalid.")

        except Exception as e:
            print(f"Error verifying signatures: {e}")
```

```
# Example usage
if __name__ == "__main__":
    num_entries = 100
    dataset_path = 'financial_data.csv'
    private_key_path = 'private_key.pem'
    public_key_path = 'public_key.pem'
    signature_path = 'dataset_signatures.npy'

    # Generate synthetic financial dataset
    df = generate_financial_data(num_entries)
    save_dataset(df, dataset_path)

    # Generate DSA keys
    generate_dsa_keys(private_key_path, public_key_path)

    # Sign dataset
    sign_dataset(private_key_path, dataset_path, signature_path)

    # Verify dataset signatures
    verify_dataset_signatures(public_key_path, dataset_path, signature_path)
```

Let's go through the code step by step, explaining each part in detail:

1. Imports

```
import pandas as pd
import numpy as np
from Crypto.PublicKey import DSA
from Crypto.Signature import DSS
from Crypto.Hash import SHA256
import datetime
import os
```

- pandas: This library is used for data manipulation and analysis. It provides data structures and functions needed to work with structured data.
- numpy: A library for numerical operations in Python. It is used here to generate random numbers and arrays.
- Crypto.PublicKey.DSA: Part of the pycryptodome library, this module is used to generate DSA (Digital Signature Algorithm) keys.
- Crypto.Signature.DSS: This module provides the tools to create and verify digital signatures using the DSA.
- Crypto.Hash.SHA256: This module allows for creating SHA-256 hashes, which are used in signing and verification processes.
- datetime: A module for manipulating dates and times.
- os: Provides a way to interact with the operating system. It's not used in this specific code but is often included for file handling and path operations.

2. Generating Synthetic Financial Data

```
def generate_financial_data(num_entries=100):
    """Generate a synthetic financial dataset with multiple columns."""
    np.random.seed(0)  # For reproducibility

    data = {
        'transaction_id': np.arange(1, num_entries + 1),
        'account_number': [f'ACCT{np.random.randint(100000, 999999)}' for _ in range(num_entries)],
        'amount': np.random.uniform(1, 10000, num_entries),
        'currency': np.random.choice(['USD', 'EUR', 'GBP'], num_entries),
        'timestamp': [datetime.datetime.now() - datetime.timedelta(days=np.random.randint(1, 365)) for _ in range(num_entries)],
        'transaction_type': np.random.choice(['credit', 'debit'], num_entries)
    }

    df = pd.DataFrame(data)
    return df
```

- np.random.seed(0): Sets the seed for the random number generator to ensure reproducibility of the generated data.
- data dictionary: Contains the columns of the dataset:
    - transaction_id: Sequential IDs for each transaction.
    - account_number: Random account numbers formatted as strings.
    - amount: Random transaction amounts between 1 and 10,000.
    - currency: Randomly chosen currency codes (USD, EUR, GBP).
    - timestamp: Random timestamps within the past year.
    - transaction_type: Randomly chosen transaction types (credit or debit).
- pd.DataFrame(data): Converts the dictionary into a pandas DataFrame, a tabular data structure.
- return df: Returns the generated DataFrame.

3. Saving the Dataset to a CSV File

```
def save_dataset(df, file_path):
    """Save the DataFrame to a CSV file."""
    df.to_csv(file_path, index=False)
    print(f"Dataset saved to {file_path}")
```

- df.to_csv(file_path, index=False): Saves the DataFrame to a CSV file at the specified path. index=False ensures that the DataFrame's index is not included in the CSV file.

- print(f"Dataset saved to {file_path}"): Prints a confirmation message indicating where the dataset has been saved.

4. Generating DSA Keys

```
def generate_dsa_keys(private_key_path, public_key_path, key_size=2048):
    """Generate DSA keys and save to files."""
    try:
        key = DSA.generate(key_size)
        private_key = key.export_key(format='PEM')
        public_key = key.publickey().export_key(format='PEM')

        with open(private_key_path, 'wb') as priv_file:
            priv_file.write(private_key)
        with open(public_key_path, 'wb') as pub_file:
            pub_file.write(public_key)

        print(f"Keys generated and saved to {private_key_path} and {public_key_path}")

    except Exception as e:
        print(f"Error generating keys: {e}")
```

- key = DSA.generate(key_size): Generates a new DSA key pair with the specified key size (2048 bits).
- private_key = key.export_key(format='PEM'): Exports the private key in PEM format, a standard format for storing cryptographic keys.
- public_key = key.publickey().export_key(format='PEM'): Exports the public key in PEM format.
- with open(private_key_path, 'wb') as priv_file: Opens the private key file in write-binary mode and writes the private key to it.
- with open(public_key_path, 'wb') as pub_file: Opens the public key file in write-binary mode and writes the public key to it.
- print(f"Keys generated and saved to {private_key_path} and {public_key_path}"): Prints a confirmation message indicating where the keys have been saved.
- except Exception as e: Catches and prints any errors that occur during key generation.

5. Signing the Dataset

```
def sign_dataset(private_key_path, data_file_path, signature_file_path):
    """Sign each entry in the dataset and save the signatures."""
    try:
        with open(private_key_path, 'rb') as key_file:
            private_key = DSA.import_key(key_file.read())

        df = pd.read_csv(data_file_path)
        signatures = []

        for index, row in df.iterrows():
            data = row.to_dict()
            data_str = str(data).encode()
            data_hash = SHA256.new(data_str)
            signer = DSS.new(private_key, 'fips-186-3')
            signature = signer.sign(data_hash)
            signatures.append(signature)

        # Save signatures
        np.save(signature_file_path, signatures)
        print(f"Signatures saved to {signature_file_path}")

    except Exception as e:
        print(f"Error signing dataset: {e}")
```

- with open(private_key_path, 'rb') as key_file: Opens the private key file in read-binary mode and imports the private key.
- df = pd.read_csv(data_file_path): Reads the dataset from the CSV file into a DataFrame.
- signatures = []: Initializes an empty list to store the signatures.
- for index, row in df.iterrows(): Iterates over each row of the DataFrame.
- data = row.to_dict(): Converts the row to a dictionary.
- data_str = str(data).encode(): Converts the dictionary to a string and encodes it to bytes.
- data_hash = SHA256.new(data_str): Creates a SHA-256 hash of the data.
- signer = DSS.new(private_key, 'fips-186-3'): Creates a new DSS signer object using the private key.
- signature = signer.sign(data_hash): Signs the hash of the data.
- signatures.append(signature): Appends the signature to the list.
- np.save(signature_file_path, signatures): Saves the list of signatures to a NumPy binary file.
- print(f"Signatures saved to {signature_file_path}"): Prints a confirmation message indicating where the signatures have been saved.

- except Exception as e: Catches and prints any errors that occur during the signing process.

6. Verifying Dataset Signatures

```
def verify_dataset_signatures(public_key_path, data_file_path, signature_file_path):
    """Verify the signatures of each entry in the dataset."""
    try:
        with open(public_key_path, 'rb') as key_file:
            public_key = DSA.import_key(key_file.read())

        df = pd.read_csv(data_file_path)
        signatures = np.load(signature_file_path)

        verifier = DSS.new(public_key, 'fips-186-3')
        for index, row in df.iterrows():
            data = row.to_dict()
            data_str = str(data).encode()
            data_hash = SHA256.new(data_str)
            signature = signatures[index]

            try:
                verifier.verify(data_hash, signature)
                print(f"Signature for entry {index + 1} is valid.")
            except (ValueError, TypeError):
                print(f"Signature for entry {index + 1} is invalid.")

    except Exception as e:
        print(f"Error verifying signatures: {e}")
```

- with open(public_key_path, 'rb') as key_file: Opens the public key file in read-binary mode and imports the public key.
- df = pd.read_csv(data_file_path): Reads the dataset from the CSV file into a DataFrame.
- signatures = np.load(signature_file_path): Loads the signatures from the NumPy binary file.
- verifier = DSS.new(public_key, 'fips-186-3'): Creates a new DSS verifier object using the public key.
- for index, row in df.iterrows(): Iterates over each row of the DataFrame.
- data = row.to_dict(): Converts the row to a dictionary.
- data_str = str(data).encode(): Converts the dictionary to a string and encodes it to bytes.
- data_hash = SHA256.new(data_str): Creates a SHA-256 hash of the data.
- signature = signatures[index]: Retrieves the signature for the current row.

- verifier.verify(data_hash, signature): Verifies the signature against the data hash.
- print(f"Signature for entry {index + 1} is valid."): Prints a message if the signature is valid.
- except (ValueError, TypeError): Catches exceptions if the verification fails and prints a message indicating the signature is invalid.
- except Exception as e: Catches and prints any errors that occur during the verification process.

7. Example Usage

```
if __name__ == "__main__":
    num_entries = 100
    dataset_path = 'financial_data.csv'
    private_key_path = 'private_key.pem'
    public_key_path = 'public_key.pem'
    signature_path = 'dataset_signatures.npy'

    # Generate synthetic financial dataset
    df = generate_financial_data(num_entries)
    save_dataset(df, dataset_path)

    # Generate DSA keys
    generate_dsa_keys(private_key_path, public_key_path)

    # Sign dataset
    sign_dataset(private_key_path, dataset_path, signature_path)

    # Verify dataset signatures
    verify_dataset_signatures(public_key_path, dataset_path, signature_path)
```

- if __name__ == "__main__":: Ensures that this code runs only when the script is executed directly, not when it is imported as a module.
- num_entries = 100: Defines the number of entries in the synthetic dataset.
- dataset_path, private_key_path, public_key_path, signature_path: Specifies file paths for saving the dataset, keys, and signatures.
- df = generate_financial_data(num_entries): Generates the synthetic dataset.
- save_dataset(df, dataset_path): Saves the generated dataset to a CSV file.
- generate_dsa_keys(private_key_path, public_key_path): Generates and saves DSA keys.
- sign_dataset(private_key_path, dataset_path, signature_path): Signs each entry in the dataset and saves the signatures.

- verify_dataset_signatures(public_key_path, dataset_path, signature_path): Verifies the signatures of each entry in the dataset.

Output

```
Dataset saved to financial_data.csv
Keys generated and saved to private_key.pem and public_key.pem
Signatures saved to dataset_signatures.npy
Signature for entry 1 is valid.
Signature for entry 2 is valid.
Signature for entry 3 is valid.
Signature for entry 4 is valid.
Signature for entry 5 is valid.
Signature for entry 6 is valid.
Signature for entry 7 is valid.
Signature for entry 8 is valid.
Signature for entry 9 is valid.
Signature for entry 10 is valid.
...
```

Project 8: GUI Tkinter for Managing Data Integrity and Security on Synthetic Financial Dataset

The purpose of this project is to create a comprehensive application for managing and verifying financial data through the use of digital signatures. The application employs a graphical user interface (GUI) built with Tkinter to streamline the processes of generating synthetic financial datasets, signing these datasets for authenticity, and verifying the signatures to ensure data integrity.

The application begins by generating synthetic financial data, which includes details such as transaction IDs, account numbers, amounts, currencies, timestamps, and transaction types. This dataset is generated with a set number of entries and saved to a CSV file. This synthetic data serves as a practical example for demonstrating the use of digital signatures in protecting and verifying financial records.

Following the generation of the dataset, the application allows users to create a pair of DSA (Digital Signature Algorithm) keys. The private key is used to sign the dataset, while the public key is used to verify these signatures. This process ensures that any modifications to the dataset can be detected, as a valid signature confirms that the data has not been tampered with since it was signed.

The core functionality of the application involves signing the generated dataset. Each entry in the dataset is signed using the private key, and these signatures are stored in a separate file. The signatures are then displayed in the GUI, providing users with a way to view and manage the cryptographic proof of the dataset's authenticity.

Verification of signatures is another critical component. Users can check whether the signatures associated with the dataset are valid using the public key. This step is crucial for ensuring that the data remains unchanged and authentic. The verification results are displayed in the GUI, showing whether each signature is valid or invalid, thereby providing immediate feedback on the integrity of the data.

The GUI itself is designed to be user-friendly and informative, featuring tabs for dataset generation, signature management, and verification results. Each tab includes a Treeview widget for displaying data with alternating row colors for improved readability. This rich interface helps users navigate the various functions of the application effectively, making the process of managing and verifying financial data straightforward and accessible.

```
import tkinter as tk
from tkinter import ttk
from tkinter import messagebox
import pandas as pd
import numpy as np
from Crypto.PublicKey import DSA
from Crypto.Signature import DSS
from Crypto.Hash import SHA256
import datetime
import os

# Functions for generating, saving, signing, and verifying data
def generate_financial_data(num_entries=100):
    np.random.seed(0)  # For reproducibility
    data = {
        'transaction_id': np.arange(1, num_entries + 1),
        'account_number': [f'ACCT{np.random.randint(100000, 999999)}' for _ in range(num_entries)],
        'amount': np.random.uniform(1, 10000, num_entries),
        'currency': np.random.choice(['USD', 'EUR', 'GBP'], num_entries),
        'timestamp': [datetime.datetime.now() - datetime.timedelta(days=np.random.randint(1, 365)) for _ in range(num_entries)],
        'transaction_type': np.random.choice(['credit', 'debit'], num_entries)
    }
    df = pd.DataFrame(data)
    return df

def save_dataset(df, file_path):
    df.to_csv(file_path, index=False)
    print(f"Dataset saved to {file_path}")
```

```python
def generate_dsa_keys(private_key_path, public_key_path, key_size=2048):
    key = DSA.generate(key_size)
    private_key = key.export_key(format='PEM')
    public_key = key.publickey().export_key(format='PEM')

    with open(private_key_path, 'wb') as priv_file:
        priv_file.write(private_key)
    with open(public_key_path, 'wb') as pub_file:
        pub_file.write(public_key)

def sign_dataset(private_key_path, data_file_path, signature_file_path):
    with open(private_key_path, 'rb') as key_file:
        private_key = DSA.import_key(key_file.read())

    df = pd.read_csv(data_file_path)
    signatures = []

    for index, row in df.iterrows():
        data = row.to_dict()
        data_str = str(data).encode()
        data_hash = SHA256.new(data_str)
        signer = DSS.new(private_key, 'fips-186-3')
        signature = signer.sign(data_hash)
        signatures.append(signature)

    np.save(signature_file_path, signatures)

def verify_dataset_signatures(public_key_path, data_file_path, signature_file_path):
    with open(public_key_path, 'rb') as key_file:
        public_key = DSA.import_key(key_file.read())

    df = pd.read_csv(data_file_path)
    signatures = np.load(signature_file_path)

    verifier = DSS.new(public_key, 'fips-186-3')
    verification_results = []

    for index, row in df.iterrows():
        data = row.to_dict()
        data_str = str(data).encode()
        data_hash = SHA256.new(data_str)
        signature = signatures[index]

        try:
            verifier.verify(data_hash, signature)
            verification_results.append(('Valid', index + 1))
        except (ValueError, TypeError):
            verification_results.append(('Invalid', index + 1))

    return verification_results

# Tkinter GUI
class DataVerificationApp(tk.Tk):
    def __init__(self):
        super().__init__()
        self.title("Data Verification App")
        self.geometry("1000x600")
```

```python
        self.create_widgets()

    def create_widgets(self):
        self.tab_control = ttk.Notebook(self)

        self.dataset_tab = ttk.Frame(self.tab_control)
        self.signatures_tab = ttk.Frame(self.tab_control)
        self.verification_tab = ttk.Frame(self.tab_control)

        self.tab_control.add(self.dataset_tab, text='Dataset')
        self.tab_control.add(self.signatures_tab, text='Signatures')
        self.tab_control.add(self.verification_tab, text='Verification Results')

        self.tab_control.pack(expand=1, fill='both')

        self.create_dataset_tab()
        self.create_signatures_tab()
        self.create_verification_tab()

    def create_dataset_tab(self):
        # Create the Treeview for displaying the dataset
        self.dataset_tree = ttk.Treeview(self.dataset_tab, columns=('transaction_id',
'account_number', 'amount', 'currency', 'timestamp', 'transaction_type'),
show='headings')
        for col in self.dataset_tree['columns']:
            self.dataset_tree.heading(col, text=col)
            self.dataset_tree.column(col, width=150, anchor='center')

        self.dataset_tree.pack(expand=1, fill='both')

        # Add a button to generate dataset
        self.generate_button = tk.Button(self.dataset_tab, text="Generate Dataset",
command=self.generate_and_display_dataset)
        self.generate_button.pack(pady=10)

    def create_signatures_tab(self):
        # Create the Treeview for displaying the signatures
        self.signatures_tree = ttk.Treeview(self.signatures_tab, columns=('index',
'signature'), show='headings')
        self.signatures_tree.heading('index', text='Index')
        self.signatures_tree.heading('signature', text='Signature')
        self.signatures_tree.column('index', width=100, anchor='center')
        self.signatures_tree.column('signature', width=500, anchor='center')

        self.signatures_tree.pack(expand=1, fill='both')

        # Add a button to generate signatures
        self.signatures_button = tk.Button(self.signatures_tab, text="Generate
Signatures", command=self.generate_and_display_signatures)
        self.signatures_button.pack(pady=10)

    def create_verification_tab(self):
        # Create the Treeview for displaying the verification results
        self.verification_tree = ttk.Treeview(self.verification_tab,
columns=('status', 'index'), show='headings')
        self.verification_tree.heading('status', text='Status')
        self.verification_tree.heading('index', text='Index')
        self.verification_tree.column('status', width=100, anchor='center')
```

```python
        self.verification_tree.column('index', width=100, anchor='center')

        self.verification_tree.pack(expand=1, fill='both')

        # Add a button to verify signatures
        self.verify_button = tk.Button(self.verification_tab, text="Verify 
Signatures", command=self.verify_and_display_signatures)
        self.verify_button.pack(pady=10)

    def generate_and_display_dataset(self):
        try:
            num_entries = 100
            self.dataset_path = 'financial_data.csv'
            df = generate_financial_data(num_entries)
            save_dataset(df, self.dataset_path)
            self.populate_tree(self.dataset_tree, df)
        except Exception as e:
            messagebox.showerror("Error", str(e))

    def generate_and_display_signatures(self):
        try:
            self.private_key_path = 'private_key.pem'
            self.signature_path = 'dataset_signatures.npy'
            sign_dataset(self.private_key_path, self.dataset_path, 
self.signature_path)

            # Load signatures
            signatures = np.load(self.signature_path)

            # Create DataFrame from signatures
            signatures_df = pd.DataFrame({
                'Index': np.arange(1, len(signatures) + 1),
                'Signature': [signature.hex() for signature in signatures]
            })

            # Populate Treeview with signatures
            self.populate_tree(self.signatures_tree, signatures_df)
        except Exception as e:
            messagebox.showerror("Error", str(e))

    def verify_and_display_signatures(self):
        try:
            self.public_key_path = 'public_key.pem'
            verification_results = verify_dataset_signatures(self.public_key_path, 
self.dataset_path, self.signature_path)

            # Create DataFrame from verification results
            verification_results_df = pd.DataFrame(verification_results, 
columns=['Index', 'Result'])

            # Populate Treeview with verification results
            self.populate_tree(self.verification_tree, verification_results_df)
        except Exception as e:
            messagebox.showerror("Error", str(e))

    def populate_tree(self, tree, df):
        for index, row in df.iterrows():
            values = tuple(row)
```

```
            tree.insert('', 'end', values=values, tags=('even' if index % 2 == 0 else
'odd'))
        tree.tag_configure('even', background='lightgray')
        tree.tag_configure('odd', background='white')
if __name__ == "__main__":
    # Generate DSA keys and save them
    private_key_path = 'private_key.pem'
    public_key_path = 'public_key.pem'
    generate_dsa_keys(private_key_path, public_key_path)

    app = DataVerificationApp()
    app.mainloop()
```

generate_financial_data(num_entries=100)

Purpose: Generates a synthetic dataset of financial transactions with a given number of entries.

Parameters:

- num_entries (int): Number of entries (rows) to generate in the dataset. Default is 100.

Detailed Steps:

1. Set Random Seed for Reproducibility:

```
np.random.seed(0)
```

- Initializes NumPy's random number generator with a seed value of 0. This ensures that the same random numbers are generated each time the function is called, making the results reproducible.

2. Create Data Dictionary:

```
data = {
    'transaction_id': np.arange(1, num_entries + 1),
    'account_number': [f'ACCT{np.random.randint(100000, 999999)}' for _ in range(num_entries)],
    'amount': np.random.uniform(1, 10000, num_entries),
    'currency': np.random.choice(['USD', 'EUR', 'GBP'], num_entries),
    'timestamp': [datetime.datetime.now() - datetime.timedelta(days=np.random.randint(1, 365)) for _ in range(num_entries)],
    'transaction_type': np.random.choice(['credit', 'debit'], num_entries)
}
```

- 'transaction_id': Creates a sequence of integers from 1 to num_entries.
- 'account_number': Generates random account numbers formatted as ACCT followed by a random 6-digit number. This is done using a list comprehension.
- 'amount': Generates a list of random amounts between 1 and 10,000 using np.random.uniform().
- 'currency': Randomly selects one of the currencies ('USD', 'EUR', 'GBP') for each entry.
- 'timestamp': Creates timestamps by subtracting a random number of days (between 1 and 365) from the current date and time.
- 'transaction_type': Randomly selects between 'credit' and 'debit' for each entry.

3. Create DataFrame:

```
df = pd.DataFrame(data)
```

- Converts the data dictionary into a Pandas DataFrame df.

4. Return DataFrame:

```
return df
```

- Returns the DataFrame df containing the generated financial data.

save_dataset(df, file_path)
Purpose: Saves the provided DataFrame to a CSV file.
Parameters:
- df (Pandas DataFrame): The DataFrame to save.
- file_path (str): Path where the CSV file will be saved.

Detailed Steps:
1. Save DataFrame to CSV:

```
df.to_csv(file_path, index=False)
```

- Writes the DataFrame df to a CSV file located at file_path. The index=False parameter excludes row indices from the CSV file.

2. Print Confirmation Message:

```
print(f"Dataset saved to {file_path}")
```

- Prints a confirmation message indicating the path where the dataset has been saved.

generate_dsa_keys(private_key_path, public_key_path, key_size=2048)
Purpose: Generates a pair of DSA (Digital Signature Algorithm) keys and saves them to specified files.
Parameters:
- private_key_path (str): File path to save the private key.
- public_key_path (str): File path to save the public key.
- key_size (int): Size of the key in bits. Default is 2048.

Detailed Steps:
1. Generate DSA Key Pair:

```
key = DSA.generate(key_size)
```

- Generates a new DSA key pair with the specified key size (2048 bits by default).

2. Export Keys:

```
private_key = key.export_key(format='PEM')
public_key = key.publickey().export_key(format='PEM')
```

- Exports the private key and public key in PEM (Privacy-Enhanced Mail) format, a standard format for storing cryptographic keys.

3. Save Private Key:

```
with open(private_key_path, 'wb') as priv_file:
    priv_file.write(private_key)
```

- Opens the file specified by private_key_path in write-binary mode and writes the private key to it.

4. Save Public Key:

```
with open(public_key_path, 'wb') as pub_file:
    pub_file.write(public_key)
```

- Opens the file specified by public_key_path in write-binary mode and writes the public key to it.

sign_dataset(private_key_path, data_file_path, signature_file_path)

Purpose: Signs each entry in a dataset using a DSA private key and saves the signatures to a file.

Parameters:
- private_key_path (str): Path to the file containing the private key.
- data_file_path (str): Path to the CSV file containing the dataset to be signed.
- signature_file_path (str): Path where the signatures will be saved.

Detailed Steps:
1. Load Private Key:

```
with open(private_key_path, 'rb') as key_file:
    private_key = DSA.import_key(key_file.read())
```

- Opens the file specified by private_key_path in read-binary mode, reads the private key, and imports it using the DSA library.

2. Load Dataset:

```
df = pd.read_csv(data_file_path)
```

- Reads the dataset from the CSV file into a Pandas DataFrame df.

3. Generate Signatures:

```
signatures = []
for index, row in df.iterrows():
    data = row.to_dict()
    data_str = str(data).encode()
    data_hash = SHA256.new(data_str)
    signer = DSS.new(private_key, 'fips-186-3')
    signature = signer.sign(data_hash)
    signatures.append(signature)
```

- Loop Through Rows: Iterates over each row of the DataFrame.
- Convert to Dictionary: Converts each row to a dictionary.
- Convert to String: Encodes the dictionary as a UTF-8 string.
- Hash Data: Hashes the string using SHA-256.
- Sign Data: Signs the hash using the DSA private key and the fips-186-3 signature scheme.
- Store Signature: Appends each signature to the signatures list.

4. Save Signatures:

```
np.save(signature_file_path, signatures)
```

- Saves the list of signatures to a file in NumPy's .npy format.

verify_dataset_signatures(public_key_path, data_file_path, signature_file_path)
Purpose: Verifies the signatures of each entry in a dataset using a DSA public key and returns the verification results.
Parameters:
- public_key_path (str): Path to the file containing the public key.
- data_file_path (str): Path to the CSV file containing the dataset to be verified.
- signature_file_path (str): Path to the file containing the signatures to be verified.

Detailed Steps:
1. Load Public Key:

```
with open(public_key_path, 'rb') as key_file:
    public_key = DSA.import_key(key_file.read())
```

- Opens the file specified by public_key_path in read-binary mode, reads the public key, and imports it using the DSA library.

2. Load Dataset and Signatures:

```
df = pd.read_csv(data_file_path)
signatures = np.load(signature_file_path)
```

- Reads the dataset from the CSV file into a Pandas DataFrame df.
- Loads the signatures from the NumPy .npy file.

3. Verify Signatures:

```
verifier = DSS.new(public_key, 'fips-186-3')
verification_results = []

for index, row in df.iterrows():
    data = row.to_dict()
    data_str = str(data).encode()
    data_hash = SHA256.new(data_str)
    signature = signatures[index]
    
    try:
        verifier.verify(data_hash, signature)
        verification_results.append(('Valid', index + 1))
    except (ValueError, TypeError):
        verification_results.append(('Invalid', index + 1))
```

- Initialize Verifier: Creates a DSA verifier object with the public key and the fips-186-3 signature scheme.
- Loop Through Rows: Iterates over each row of the DataFrame.
- Convert to Dictionary: Converts each row to a dictionary.
- Convert to String: Encodes the dictionary as a UTF-8 string.
- Hash Data: Hashes the string using SHA-256.
- Get Signature: Retrieves the signature for the current row from the signatures list.
- Verify Signature: Attempts to verify the signature using the public key. If successful, appends ('Valid', index + 1) to the results; otherwise, appends ('Invalid', index + 1).

4. Return Results:

   ```
   return verification_results
   ```

   - Returns a list of tuples where each tuple contains the verification result ('Valid' or 'Invalid') and the row number.

Here's the explanation of each function in the DataVerificationApp class:

__init__(self)

```
def __init__(self):
    super().__init__()
    self.title("Data Verification App")
    self.geometry("1000x600")
    self.create_widgets()
```

- Purpose: Initializes the main window of the application.
- Details:
  - super().__init__() calls the initializer of the parent class tk.Tk, setting up the Tkinter application window.
  - self.title("Data Verification App") sets the title of the window to "Data Verification App".
  - self.geometry("1000x600") defines the size of the window as 1000 pixels wide by 600 pixels tall.
  - self.create_widgets() is called to set up the user interface elements of the application.

create_widgets(self)

```
def create_widgets(self):
    self.tab_control = ttk.Notebook(self)

    self.dataset_tab = ttk.Frame(self.tab_control)
    self.signatures_tab = ttk.Frame(self.tab_control)
    self.verification_tab = ttk.Frame(self.tab_control)

    self.tab_control.add(self.dataset_tab, text='Dataset')
    self.tab_control.add(self.signatures_tab, text='Signatures')
    self.tab_control.add(self.verification_tab, text='Verification Results')
```

```
self.tab_control.pack(expand=1, fill='both')

self.create_dataset_tab()
self.create_signatures_tab()
self.create_verification_tab()
```

- Purpose: Creates and configures the main components of the GUI.
- Details:
    - self.tab_control = ttk.Notebook(self) creates a tabbed notebook widget to hold different tabs.
    - self.dataset_tab, self.signatures_tab, and self.verification_tab are frames to be used as individual tabs in the notebook.
    - self.tab_control.add(self.dataset_tab, text='Dataset') adds the dataset tab to the notebook with the label "Dataset".
    - self.tab_control.pack(expand=1, fill='both') places the notebook widget in the window, allowing it to expand and fill available space.
    - Calls self.create_dataset_tab(), self.create_signatures_tab(), and self.create_verification_tab() to populate each tab with widgets.

create_dataset_tab(self)

```
def create_dataset_tab(self):
    self.dataset_tree = ttk.Treeview(self.dataset_tab, columns=('transaction_id',
'account_number', 'amount', 'currency', 'timestamp', 'transaction_type'),
show='headings')
    for col in self.dataset_tree['columns']:
        self.dataset_tree.heading(col, text=col)
        self.dataset_tree.column(col, width=150, anchor='center')

    self.dataset_tree.pack(expand=1, fill='both')

    self.generate_button = tk.Button(self.dataset_tab, text="Generate Dataset",
command=self.generate_and_display_dataset)
    self.generate_button.pack(pady=10)
```

- Purpose: Sets up the "Dataset" tab with a Treeview and a button.
- Details:
    - self.dataset_tree = ttk.Treeview(self.dataset_tab, columns=('transaction_id', 'account_number', 'amount', 'currency', 'timestamp', 'transaction_type'), show='headings') creates a Treeview widget in the dataset tab with specified columns and no extra decorations (show='headings').

- for col in self.dataset_tree['columns']: loops through each column name to set up column headings and widths.
- self.dataset_tree.heading(col, text=col) sets the heading of each column.
- self.dataset_tree.column(col, width=150, anchor='center') sets the width and alignment for each column.
- self.dataset_tree.pack(expand=1, fill='both') places the Treeview in the tab, allowing it to expand and fill the space.
- self.generate_button = tk.Button(self.dataset_tab, text="Generate Dataset", command=self.generate_and_display_dataset) creates a button labeled "Generate Dataset" that triggers self.generate_and_display_dataset when clicked.
- self.generate_button.pack(pady=10) places the button in the tab with padding around it.

create_signatures_tab(self)

```
def create_signatures_tab(self):
    self.signatures_tree = ttk.Treeview(self.signatures_tab, columns=('index',
'signature'), show='headings')
    self.signatures_tree.heading('index', text='Index')
    self.signatures_tree.heading('signature', text='Signature')
    self.signatures_tree.column('index', width=100, anchor='center')
    self.signatures_tree.column('signature', width=500, anchor='center')

    self.signatures_tree.pack(expand=1, fill='both')

    self.signatures_button = tk.Button(self.signatures_tab, text="Generate
Signatures", command=self.generate_and_display_signatures)
    self.signatures_button.pack(pady=10)
```

- Purpose: Sets up the "Signatures" tab with a Treeview and a button.
- Details:
    - self.signatures_tree = ttk.Treeview(self.signatures_tab, columns=('index', 'signature'), show='headings') creates a Treeview widget in the signatures tab with columns for index and signature.
    - self.signatures_tree.heading('index', text='Index') sets the heading for the index column.
    - self.signatures_tree.heading('signature', text='Signature') sets the heading for the signature column.

- self.signatures_tree.column('index', width=100, anchor='center') sets the width and alignment for the index column.
- self.signatures_tree.column('signature', width=500, anchor='center') sets the width and alignment for the signature column.
- self.signatures_tree.pack(expand=1, fill='both') places the Treeview in the tab, allowing it to expand and fill the space.
- self.signatures_button = tk.Button(self.signatures_tab, text="Generate Signatures", command=self.generate_and_display_signatures) creates a button labeled "Generate Signatures" that triggers self.generate_and_display_signatures when clicked.
- self.signatures_button.pack(pady=10) places the button in the tab with padding around it.

create_verification_tab(self)

```
def create_verification_tab(self):
    self.verification_tree = ttk.Treeview(self.verification_tab, columns=('status', 'index'), show='headings')
    self.verification_tree.heading('status', text='Status')
    self.verification_tree.heading('index', text='Index')
    self.verification_tree.column('status', width=100, anchor='center')
    self.verification_tree.column('index', width=100, anchor='center')

    self.verification_tree.pack(expand=1, fill='both')

    self.verify_button = tk.Button(self.verification_tab, text="Verify Signatures", command=self.verify_and_display_signatures)
    self.verify_button.pack(pady=10)
```

- Purpose: Sets up the "Verification Results" tab with a Treeview and a button.
- Details:
  - self.verification_tree = ttk.Treeview(self.verification_tab, columns=('status', 'index'), show='headings') creates a Treeview widget in the verification results tab with columns for status and index.
  - self.verification_tree.heading('status', text='Status') sets the heading for the status column.
  - self.verification_tree.heading('index', text='Index') sets the heading for the index column.
  - self.verification_tree.column('status', width=100, anchor='center') sets the width and alignment for the status column.

- self.verification_tree.column('index', width=100, anchor='center') sets the width and alignment for the index column.
- self.verification_tree.pack(expand=1, fill='both') places the Treeview in the tab, allowing it to expand and fill the space.
- self.verify_button = tk.Button(self.verification_tab, text="Verify Signatures", command=self.verify_and_display_signatures) creates a button labeled "Verify Signatures" that triggers self.verify_and_display_signatures when clicked.
- self.verify_button.pack(pady=10) places the button in the tab with padding around it.

generate_and_display_dataset(self)

```
def generate_and_display_dataset(self):
    try:
        num_entries = 100
        self.dataset_path = 'financial_data.csv'
        df = generate_financial_data(num_entries)
        save_dataset(df, self.dataset_path)
        self.populate_tree(self.dataset_tree, df)
    except Exception as e:
        messagebox.showerror("Error", str(e))
```

- Purpose: Generates a financial dataset and displays it in the "Dataset" tab.
- Details:
    - num_entries = 100 specifies the number of entries for the dataset.
    - self.dataset_path = 'financial_data.csv' sets the file path where the dataset will be saved.
    - df = generate_financial_data(num_entries) calls the function to generate a DataFrame with financial data.
    - save_dataset(df, self.dataset_path) saves the generated DataFrame to a CSV file.
    - self.populate_tree(self.dataset_tree, df) populates the Treeview in the "Dataset" tab with the data from the DataFrame.
    - If any error occurs, an error message is displayed using messagebox.showerror.

generate_and_display_signatures(self)

```
def generate_and_display_signatures(self):
    try:
        self.private_key_path = 'private_key.pem'
        self.signature_path = 'dataset_signatures.npy'
        sign_dataset(self.private_key_path, self.dataset_path, self.signature_path)

        signatures = np.load(self.signature_path)
        signatures_df = pd.DataFrame({
            'Index': np.arange(1, len(signatures) + 1),
            'Signature': [signature.hex() for signature in signatures]
        })

        self.populate_tree(self.signatures_tree, signatures_df)
    except Exception as e:
        messagebox.showerror("Error", str(e))
```

- Purpose: Generates and displays digital signatures for the dataset in the "Signatures" tab.
- Details:
    - self.private_key_path = 'private_key.pem' specifies the path to the private key used for signing.
    - self.signature_path = 'dataset_signatures.npy' specifies the path where the signatures will be saved.
    - sign_dataset(self.private_key_path, self.dataset_path, self.signature_path) generates signatures for the dataset.
    - signatures = np.load(self.signature_path) loads the saved signatures from the file.
    - signatures_df = pd.DataFrame({ 'Index': np.arange(1, len(signatures) + 1), 'Signature': [signature.hex() for signature in signatures] }) creates a DataFrame with indices and hexadecimal representations of the signatures.
    - self.populate_tree(self.signatures_tree, signatures_df) populates the Treeview in the "Signatures" tab with the signatures.
    - If any error occurs, an error message is displayed using messagebox.showerror.

verify_and_display_signatures(self)

```
def verify_and_display_signatures(self):
    try:
        self.public_key_path = 'public_key.pem'
```

```
        verification_results = verify_dataset_signatures(self.public_key_path,
self.dataset_path, self.signature_path)
        verification_results_df = pd.DataFrame(verification_results,
columns=['Index', 'Result'])
        self.populate_tree(self.verification_tree, verification_results_df)
    except Exception as e:
        messagebox.showerror("Error", str(e))
```

- Purpose: Verifies the digital signatures and displays the results in the "Verification Results" tab.
- Details:
    - self.public_key_path = 'public_key.pem' specifies the path to the public key used for verification.
    - verification_results = verify_dataset_signatures(self.public_key_path, self.dataset_path, self.signature_path) verifies the signatures against the dataset.
    - verification_results_df = pd.DataFrame(verification_results, columns=['Index', 'Result']) creates a DataFrame with verification results.
    - self.populate_tree(self.verification_tree, verification_results_df) populates the Treeview in the "Verification Results" tab with the verification results.
    - If any error occurs, an error message is displayed using messagebox.showerror.

populate_tree(self, tree, df)

```
def populate_tree(self, tree, df):
    for index, row in df.iterrows():
        values = tuple(row)
        tree.insert('', 'end', values=values, tags=('even' if index % 2 == 0 else 'odd'))
    tree.tag_configure('even', background='lightgray')
    tree.tag_configure('odd', background='white')
```

- Purpose: Populates a Treeview widget with data from a DataFrame.
- Details:
    - for index, row in df.iterrows(): iterates through each row of the DataFrame.
    - values = tuple(row) converts the row data into a tuple of values.

- tree.insert(", 'end', values=values, tags=('even' if index % 2 == 0 else 'odd')) inserts the values into the Treeview. Rows are tagged as 'even' or 'odd' for alternating row colors.
- tree.tag_configure('even', background='lightgray') sets the background color for even rows to light gray.
- tree.tag_configure('odd', background='white') sets the background color for odd rows to white.

Project 9: Hiding Confidential Message with DSA and LSB Steganography

This code integrates Digital Signature Algorithm (DSA) with Least Significant Bit (LSB) steganography to hide a signed confidential message within an image. The code first defines helper functions to convert text to bits and vice versa, which is crucial for embedding the message within the pixel data of the image. DSA keys are generated and stored in files, allowing for the signing and verification of data. The signature is encoded in Base64 to ensure it can be easily embedded and transmitted. The generate_dsa_keys function creates and saves both the private and public keys, while the sign_data function signs the message using the private key, ensuring authenticity and integrity of the data. The verify_data function validates the authenticity of the message using the public key.

In the next step, the code uses LSB steganography to hide the signed message inside an image. The embed_data_in_image function modifies the least significant bits of the red channel of each pixel to embed the binary representation of the message and its signature. The text_to_bits function converts the message and signature to a series of bits, which are then embedded within the image pixels. Once the message is fully embedded, the modified image is saved as a new image file. To retrieve the hidden data, the extract_data_from_image function extracts the least significant bits from the red channel of the image's pixels, reconstructing the hidden message bit by bit.

Finally, in the main function, the process is demonstrated by generating DSA keys, signing a financial transaction message, embedding the signed message into an image, and then extracting it from the image. The extracted message is then verified using the public DSA key, ensuring that the message hasn't been altered and confirming its authenticity. This example showcases a practical application of combining cryptographic signing with steganography to protect the confidentiality and integrity of sensitive information hidden in an image file.

```python
from PIL import Image
from Crypto.PublicKey import DSA
from Crypto.Signature import DSS
from Crypto.Hash import SHA256
import base64
import os

# Helper function to convert text to bits
def text_to_bits(text):
    bits = []
    for char in text:
        bits.extend([int(bit) for bit in format(ord(char), '08b')])
    return bits
```

```python
# Helper function to convert bits to text
def bits_to_text(bits):
    chars = []
    for i in range(0, len(bits), 8):
        byte = bits[i:i + 8]
        byte_str = ''.join([str(bit) for bit in byte])
        chars.append(chr(int(byte_str, 2)))
    return ''.join(chars)

# Generate DSA keys and save them to files
def generate_dsa_keys(private_key_path, public_key_path):
    key = DSA.generate(2048)
    private_key = key.export_key()
    public_key = key.publickey().export_key()

    with open(private_key_path, 'wb') as priv_file:
        priv_file.write(private_key)

    with open(public_key_path, 'wb') as pub_file:
        pub_file.write(public_key)

    print("DSA keys generated.")

# Sign data with the private DSA key
def sign_data(private_key_path, data):
    with open(private_key_path, 'rb') as key_file:
        private_key = DSA.import_key(key_file.read())

    hash_obj = SHA256.new(data.encode())
    signer = DSS.new(private_key, 'fips-186-3')
    signature = signer.sign(hash_obj)

    # Encode signature as base64 for embedding
    signature_base64 = base64.b64encode(signature).decode()
    print("Data signed.")
    return signature_base64

# Verify the data with the public DSA key
def verify_data(public_key_path, data, signature_base64):
    with open(public_key_path, 'rb') as key_file:
        public_key = DSA.import_key(key_file.read())

    hash_obj = SHA256.new(data.encode())
    verifier = DSS.new(public_key, 'fips-186-3')

    signature = base64.b64decode(signature_base64)

    try:
        verifier.verify(hash_obj, signature)
        print("Signature is valid.")
    except ValueError:
        print("Signature is invalid.")

# Embed data in image using LSB steganography
def embed_data_in_image(image_path, output_image_path, data_to_hide):
    img = Image.open(image_path)
    pixels = list(img.getdata())
```

```python
    data_bits = text_to_bits(data_to_hide)
    data_len = len(data_bits)
    data_index = 0

    new_pixels = []

    for pixel in pixels:
        if data_index < data_len:
            r, g, b = pixel[:3]
            r = (r & ~1) | data_bits[data_index]  # Change the least significant bit of red channel
            data_index += 1
            new_pixels.append((r, g, b))
        else:
            new_pixels.append(pixel)

    img.putdata(new_pixels)
    img.save(output_image_path)
    print(f"Data embedded in {output_image_path}")

# Extract data from image using LSB steganography
def extract_data_from_image(image_path, data_size_in_bits):
    img = Image.open(image_path)
    pixels = list(img.getdata())

    data_bits = []

    for pixel in pixels[:data_size_in_bits]:  # Only extract the number of bits we know exist
        r, g, b = pixel[:3]
        data_bits.append(r & 1)  # Extract the LSB from red channel

    extracted_data = bits_to_text(data_bits)
    return extracted_data

# Main function to demonstrate the process
def main():
    # Key paths
    private_key_path = 'private_key.pem'
    public_key_path = 'public_key.pem'

    # Step 1: Generate DSA keys
    generate_dsa_keys(private_key_path, public_key_path)

    # Step 2: Message to hide and sign
    confidential_message = "Financial Transaction Report: Total= $5000"

    # Step 3: Sign the message
    signed_data = sign_data(private_key_path, confidential_message)

    # Prepare data with signature for embedding
    data_to_hide = confidential_message + "\nSignature: " + signed_data

    # Step 4: Embed signed data into image
    embed_data_in_image("input_image.png", "image_with_hidden_data.png", data_to_hide)

    # Step 5: Extract the hidden data from the image
```

```
    extracted_data_with_signature = 
extract_data_from_image("image_with_hidden_data.png", 
len(text_to_bits(data_to_hide)))

    # Separate the extracted data from the signature
    extracted_data, extracted_signature = 
extracted_data_with_signature.rsplit("\nSignature: ", 1)

    print(f"Extracted Data: {extracted_data}")
    print(f"Extracted Signature: {extracted_signature}")

    # Step 6: Verify the extracted data
    verify_data(public_key_path, extracted_data, extracted_signature)

if __name__ == "__main__":
    main()
```

text_to_bits() Function

The text_to_bits() function takes a string of text and converts each character in the text into its binary representation, which is then flattened into a list of bits (0s and 1s). This list of bits is often used in applications involving data manipulation, such as data embedding or encryption.

```
def text_to_bits(text):
    bits = []
    for char in text:
        bits.extend([int(bit) for bit in format(ord(char), '08b')])
    return bits
```

1. Function Definition

```
def text_to_bits(text):
```

- Purpose: Defines a function named text_to_bits. It takes one parameter text, which is expected to be a string. The function will convert this string into a list of bits.

2. Initialize an Empty List

```
    bits = []
```

- Purpose: Creates an empty list named bits that will be used to store the binary representation of each character from the input string. This list will eventually contain a sequence of bits (0s and 1s).

3. Iterate Over Each Character

```
for char in text:
```

- Purpose: Starts a loop that iterates over each character in the input string text. The variable char represents the current character in each iteration of the loop.

4. Convert Character to Binary Representation

```
bits.extend([int(bit) for bit in format(ord(char), '08b')])
```

Explanation:
1. ord(char):
    - Purpose: Converts the character char into its corresponding ASCII integer value. For example, ord('A') returns 65, which is the ASCII value for the character 'A'.
    - Detail: ord() is a built-in Python function that returns an integer representing the Unicode code point of a given character. For characters in the ASCII range, it returns the ASCII code.
2. format(..., '08b'):
    - Purpose: Converts the ASCII integer value into an 8-bit binary string.
    - Detail: format() is a Python function used to format values. The format specifier '08b' means to convert the integer into an 8-bit binary number, padding with leading zeros if necessary. For example, format(65, '08b') results in the string '01000001', which is the 8-bit binary representation of 65 (ASCII for 'A').
3. [int(bit) for bit in format(...)]:
    - Purpose: Converts each character in the binary string (which is currently a string) into an integer.
    - Detail: This is a list comprehension that iterates over each character in the binary string (e.g., '0' or '1') and converts it into an integer (0 or 1). For instance, '01000001' becomes [0, 1, 0, 0, 0, 0, 0, 1].
4. bits.extend(...):
    - Purpose: Adds the list of bits obtained from the current character to the bits list.

- Detail: extend() is used to append the elements of the provided list to bits. This is different from append(), which would add the entire list as a single element. Using extend(), each bit is added individually to the bits list.

5. *Return the List of Bits*

```
return bits
```

- Purpose: After processing all characters in the input string, the function returns the complete list of bits.

Example Walkthrough
Let's consider an example where the input string is "AB".
1. Convert 'A' to Binary:
    - ord('A') returns 65.
    - format(65, '08b') results in '01000001'.
    - Convert '01000001' to a list of integers: [0, 1, 0, 0, 0, 0, 0, 1].
2. Convert 'B' to Binary:
    - ord('B') returns 66.
    - format(66, '08b') results in '01000010'.
    - Convert '01000010' to a list of integers: [0, 1, 0, 0, 0, 0, 1, 0].
3. Combine Lists:
    - Combine the two lists: [0, 1, 0, 0, 0, 0, 0, 1] + [0, 1, 0, 0, 0, 0, 1, 0].
    - The final list is [0, 1, 0, 0, 0, 0, 0, 1, 0, 1, 0, 0, 0, 0, 1, 0].

Summary
The text_to_bits() function is a useful utility for converting a string into its binary representation. Each character is translated into its ASCII value, which is then formatted as an 8-bit binary string. This binary string is further broken down into individual bits, and all bits are collected into a single list. This list of bits can be used for further processing, such as embedding data into an image or performing encryption.

bits_to_text() Function

The bits_to_text() function takes a list of bits (0s and 1s) and converts it back into a string of text. Each character in the text is represented by a sequence of 8 bits (one byte), and the function reconstructs these characters from their binary representations.

```
def bits_to_text(bits):
    chars = []
    for i in range(0, len(bits), 8):
        byte = bits[i:i + 8]
        byte_str = ''.join([str(bit) for bit in byte])
        chars.append(chr(int(byte_str, 2)))
    return ''.join(chars)
```

1. Function Definition

```
def bits_to_text(bits):
```

- Purpose: Defines a function named bits_to_text. It takes one parameter, bits, which is expected to be a list of integers (0s and 1s) representing the binary form of the text. The function will convert these bits back into a readable text string.

2. Initialize an Empty List

```
chars = []
```

- Purpose: Creates an empty list named chars that will be used to store the characters reconstructed from the binary data. Each character is processed individually and added to this list.

3. Iterate Over Bits in Chunks of 8

```
for i in range(0, len(bits), 8):
```

- Purpose: Starts a loop that iterates over the list of bits in chunks of 8 bits (one byte at a time).
- Detail: range(0, len(bits), 8) generates a sequence of indices starting from 0 to the length of bits, with a step size of 8. This way, the loop processes the bits in blocks of 8.

4. Extract a Byte of Bits

```
byte = bits[i:i + 8]
```

- Purpose: Slices the bits list to get a chunk of 8 bits. This represents one byte of data.
- Detail: bits[i:i + 8] extracts a sublist from index i to i + 8, which contains the next 8 bits. For example, if i is 0, byte would be bits[0:8].

5. Convert Byte to String

```
byte_str = ''.join([str(bit) for bit in byte])
```

- Purpose: Converts the list of bits (integers) into a binary string representation.
- Detail:
  - List Comprehension: [str(bit) for bit in byte] iterates over each bit in the byte list, converts it to a string, and collects these string representations into a new list.
  - ''.join(...): Joins the elements of the list into a single string. For example, [0, 1, 0, 0, 0, 0, 0, 1] becomes '01000001'.

6. Convert Binary String to Character

```
chars.append(chr(int(byte_str, 2)))
```

- Purpose: Converts the binary string into its corresponding ASCII character and appends it to the chars list.
- Detail:
  - int(byte_str, 2): Converts the binary string byte_str to an integer using base 2. For example, '01000001' becomes 65.
  - chr(...): Converts the integer into its corresponding ASCII character. For example, 65 becomes 'A'.
  - chars.append(...): Adds the character to the chars list.

7. Return the Reconstructed Text

```
return ''.join(chars)
```

- Purpose: Joins all characters in the chars list into a single string and returns it.
- Detail: ''.join(chars) concatenates the list of characters into one continuous string. For example, if chars contains ['A', 'B'], the result is 'AB'.

Example Walkthrough

Let's consider an example with a list of bits representing the string "AB":
1. Input Bits: [0, 1, 0, 0, 0, 0, 0, 1, 0, 1, 0, 0, 0, 0, 1, 0] (binary representation of "AB").
2. Processing First Byte:
   - byte = [0, 1, 0, 0, 0, 0, 0, 1] (binary for 'A').
   - byte_str = '01000001'.
   - int(byte_str, 2) converts '01000001' to 65.
   - chr(65) gives 'A'.
   - Append 'A' to chars.
3. Processing Second Byte:
   - byte = [0, 1, 0, 0, 0, 0, 1, 0] (binary for 'B').
   - byte_str = '01000010'.
   - int(byte_str, 2) converts '01000010' to 66.
   - chr(66) gives 'B'.
   - Append 'B' to chars.
4. Final Result:
   - chars becomes ['A', 'B'].
   - ''.join(chars) gives 'AB'.

Summary

The bits_to_text() function reconstructs a string from a list of binary bits. It processes the bits in 8-bit chunks, converts each chunk from binary to an integer, then to a character, and finally combines all characters into a string. This function is useful for reversing the conversion of text to binary format, enabling applications such as decoding data that was encoded for storage or transmission.

generate_dsa_keys() Function
Function Definition

```
def generate_dsa_keys(private_key_path, public_key_path):
```

- Purpose: Defines a function named generate_dsa_keys. It takes two parameters: private_key_path and public_key_path, which are the file paths where the private and public keys will be saved, respectively.

Key Generation

```
key = DSA.generate(2048)
```

- Purpose: Generates a new pair of DSA keys.
- Detail:
    - DSA.generate(2048): This method from the Crypto.PublicKey.DSA module generates a new DSA key pair with a key size of 2048 bits. A larger key size provides more security but requires more computational resources. DSA keys typically come in sizes such as 1024, 2048, or 3072 bits. The generated key object contains both the private and public components of the key pair.

Export Keys

```
private_key = key.export_key()
public_key = key.publickey().export_key()
```

- Purpose: Extracts and prepares the private and public keys for saving.
- Detail:
    - key.export_key(): This method exports the private key in a serialized format. It typically returns a byte string representing the private key.
    - key.publickey().export_key(): This method first retrieves the public key component from the key object using key.publickey(), and then exports it in a serialized format, similar to the private key. The public key is used to verify signatures created with the corresponding private key.

Save Keys to Files

```
with open(private_key_path, 'wb') as priv_file:
    priv_file.write(private_key)
```

- Purpose: Saves the private key to a file.
- Detail:
    - with open(private_key_path, 'wb') as priv_file:: Opens the file specified by private_key_path in binary write mode ('wb'). This ensures that the file is handled as a binary file, which is necessary for saving cryptographic keys.
    - priv_file.write(private_key): Writes the serialized private key data to the file.

```
with open(public_key_path, 'wb') as pub_file:
    pub_file.write(public_key)
```

- Purpose: Saves the public key to a file.
- Detail:
    - with open(public_key_path, 'wb') as pub_file:: Opens the file specified by public_key_path in binary write mode ('wb').
    - pub_file.write(public_key): Writes the serialized public key data to the file.

Print Confirmation

```
print("DSA keys generated.")
```

- Purpose: Outputs a confirmation message to indicate that the key generation process has been completed successfully. This is useful for providing feedback to the user or for debugging purposes.

Summary

The generate_dsa_keys() function performs the following tasks:
1. Generates a new pair of DSA keys with a key size of 2048 bits.
2. Exports the private and public keys in a serialized format.
3. Saves the private key to a file specified by private_key_path and the public key to a file specified by public_key_path.

4. Prints a confirmation message indicating that the keys have been generated and saved.

This function is crucial in cryptographic applications where secure key management is required for tasks such as digital signatures, data encryption, or secure communication.

sign_data() Function
Function Definition

```
def sign_data(private_key_path, data):
```

- Purpose: Defines a function named sign_data. It takes two parameters: private_key_path (the file path where the private key is stored) and data (the data to be signed).

Load Private Key

```
with open(private_key_path, 'rb') as key_file:
    private_key = DSA.import_key(key_file.read())
```

- Purpose: Loads the private key from a file and imports it into a DSA key object.
- Detail:
    - with open(private_key_path, 'rb') as key_file:: Opens the file specified by private_key_path in binary read mode ('rb'). This mode ensures that the file is read as binary data, which is necessary for handling cryptographic keys.
    - key_file.read(): Reads the entire contents of the file into a byte string.
    - DSA.import_key(): Takes the byte string and converts it into a DSA key object that can be used for signing. This method parses the key data and creates an object that represents the private key.

Hash the Data

```
hash_obj = SHA256.new(data.encode())
```

- Purpose: Creates a SHA-256 hash of the data to be signed.

- Detail:
    - data.encode(): Converts the input data from a string into bytes using the default UTF-8 encoding. Cryptographic hash functions work on byte data, so encoding is necessary.
    - SHA256.new(): Initializes a new SHA-256 hash object with the byte-encoded data. This hash object will be used to compute the hash value, which is the input for the signature process.

Sign the Data

```
signer = DSS.new(private_key, 'fips-186-3')
signature = signer.sign(hash_obj)
```

- Purpose: Signs the hashed data using the private DSA key.
- Detail:
    - DSS.new(private_key, 'fips-186-3'): Creates a new DSS (Digital Signature Standard) signer object using the private key and the 'fips-186-3' signing scheme. 'fips-186-3' specifies the DSA standard for signatures.
    - signer.sign(hash_obj): Signs the hash object containing the SHA-256 hash of the data. This generates the digital signature, which is a byte string representing the signature for the hashed data.

Encode Signature as Base64

```
signature_base64 = base64.b64encode(signature).decode()
```

- Purpose: Encodes the binary signature into a Base64 string for easier handling and embedding.
- Detail:
    - base64.b64encode(signature): Encodes the binary signature into a Base64-encoded byte string. Base64 encoding is used to represent binary data in an ASCII string format, which is useful for embedding the signature in text-based formats or data.
    - .decode(): Converts the Base64-encoded byte string into a standard string (text) format.

Print Confirmation and Return

```
print("Data signed.")
return signature_base64
```

- Purpose: Prints a confirmation message and returns the Base64-encoded signature.
- Detail:
    - print("Data signed."): Outputs a message to the console indicating that the data has been successfully signed.
    - return signature_base64: Returns the Base64-encoded signature to the caller. This allows the signature to be used for further operations, such as embedding in a file or verifying later.

Summary

The sign_data() function:
1. Loads the private DSA key from a specified file.
2. Hashes the input data using SHA-256.
3. Signs the hash with the private DSA key to generate a digital signature.
4. Encodes the binary signature in Base64 format for easier handling.
5. Prints a confirmation message and returns the Base64-encoded signature.

This function is critical in cryptographic applications where data integrity and authenticity are important. It ensures that the data can be verified later using the corresponding public key.

verify_data() Function

The verify_data() function is designed to verify the authenticity of data using a public DSA (Digital Signature Algorithm) key and a digital signature. Here is a detailed breakdown of each part of this function:

Function Definition

```
def verify_data(public_key_path, data, signature_base64):
```

- Purpose: Defines a function named verify_data that takes three parameters:
    - public_key_path: The file path where the public DSA key is stored.

- data: The data to verify.
- signature_base64: The Base64-encoded digital signature to verify against the data.

Load Public Key

```
with open(public_key_path, 'rb') as key_file:
    public_key = DSA.import_key(key_file.read())
```

- Purpose: Loads the public key from a file and imports it into a DSA key object.
- Detail:
    - with open(public_key_path, 'rb') as key_file:: Opens the file specified by public_key_path in binary read mode ('rb'). This ensures that the file is read as binary data, which is necessary for handling cryptographic keys.
    - key_file.read(): Reads the entire contents of the file into a byte string.
    - DSA.import_key(): Converts the byte string into a DSA key object that represents the public key. This object is used for verifying signatures.

Hash the Data

```
hash_obj = SHA256.new(data.encode())
```

- Purpose: Creates a SHA-256 hash of the data to be verified.
- Detail:
    - data.encode(): Converts the input data from a string into bytes using UTF-8 encoding. Cryptographic hash functions operate on byte data.
    - SHA256.new(): Initializes a new SHA-256 hash object with the byte-encoded data. This hash object will be used to compare against the hash of the data that was originally signed.

Initialize Verifier

```
verifier = DSS.new(public_key, 'fips-186-3')
```

- Purpose: Creates a new DSS verifier object using the public key and the 'fips-186-3' signature scheme.
- Detail:
    - DSS.new(public_key, 'fips-186-3'): Initializes a verifier object that will use the specified public key and signature scheme ('fips-186-3'), which corresponds to the DSA standard for signature verification.

Decode Signature

```
signature = base64.b64decode(signature_base64)
```

- Purpose: Decodes the Base64-encoded signature back into its binary form.
- Detail:
    - base64.b64decode(signature_base64): Decodes the Base64-encoded signature into the original binary format. Base64 encoding is used for safe representation of binary data in text form, so it must be decoded to obtain the original signature.

Verify the Signature

```
try:
    verifier.verify(hash_obj, signature)
    print("Signature is valid.")
except ValueError:
    print("Signature is invalid.")
```

- Purpose: Verifies the signature against the data hash using the public key.
- Detail:
    - verifier.verify(hash_obj, signature): Attempts to verify the signature using the hash of the data and the decoded signature. If the signature is valid and matches the hash, the verification is successful.
    - try block: Encapsulates the verification attempt to handle potential exceptions.
    - except ValueError: Catches a ValueError exception if the signature verification fails. This exception is raised if the signature does not match the expected hash value, indicating that the signature is invalid.

- print("Signature is valid."): If the signature is valid, this message is printed.
- print("Signature is invalid."): If the signature is invalid, this message is printed.

Summary

The verify_data() function:
1. Loads the public DSA key from a specified file.
2. Hashes the input data using SHA-256 to obtain a hash object.
3. Initializes a DSA verifier object with the public key and the signature scheme.
4. Decodes the Base64-encoded signature back into binary format.
5. Verifies the signature against the hash of the data. If verification fails, it prints an error message; otherwise, it confirms that the signature is valid.

This function is crucial for ensuring the integrity and authenticity of data, verifying that the data has not been tampered with and that the signature was generated by the corresponding private key.

embed_data_in_image() Function

The embed_data_in_image() function uses Least Significant Bit (LSB) steganography to hide data within an image. This technique involves manipulating the least significant bits of the pixel values to embed data without significantly altering the visual appearance of the image. Here's a detailed breakdown of each part of this function:

Function Definition

```
def embed_data_in_image(image_path, output_image_path, data_to_hide):
```

- Purpose: Defines a function named embed_data_in_image that takes three parameters:
  - image_path: The file path of the image in which data will be embedded.
  - output_image_path: The file path where the modified image with the hidden data will be saved.
  - data_to_hide: The data that needs to be embedded in the image.

Open Image and Extract Pixels

```
img = Image.open(image_path)
pixels = list(img.getdata())
```

- Purpose: Opens the specified image and retrieves its pixel data.
- Detail:
    - Image.open(image_path): Opens the image file specified by image_path. The Image class from the PIL (Python Imaging Library) is used to handle image files.
    - img.getdata(): Retrieves the pixel data of the image. Each pixel is represented as a tuple (or a list) of RGB values (Red, Green, Blue).
    - list(img.getdata()): Converts the pixel data into a list of tuples. This makes it easier to manipulate individual pixel values.

Convert Data to Bits

```
data_bits = text_to_bits(data_to_hide)
data_len = len(data_bits)
data_index = 0
```

- Purpose: Converts the data to be hidden into a list of bits and initializes an index for processing these bits.
- Detail:
    - text_to_bits(data_to_hide): Calls the text_to_bits function (described earlier) to convert the data into a list of bits.
    - data_len: Stores the total number of bits in the data_bits list.
    - data_index: Initializes an index to keep track of which bit is being processed.

Process Pixels and Embed Data

```
new_pixels = []

for pixel in pixels:
    if data_index < data_len:
        r, g, b = pixel[:3]
        r = (r & ~1) | data_bits[data_index]  # Change the least significant bit
of red channel
```

```
        data_index += 1
        new_pixels.append((r, g, b))
    else:
        new_pixels.append(pixel)
```

- Purpose: Iterates over each pixel, modifies the least significant bit (LSB) of the red channel to hide the data bits, and collects the modified pixels.
- Detail:
    - new_pixels = []: Initializes an empty list to store the modified pixels.
    - for pixel in pixels:: Loops through each pixel in the image.
    - if data_index < data_len:: Checks if there are still bits left to embed.
        - r, g, b = pixel[:3]: Extracts the red, green, and blue values from the pixel tuple. Only the red channel is modified.
        - r = (r & ~1) | data_bits[data_index]: Modifies the least significant bit of the red channel to hide a bit of data:
            - r & ~1: Clears the LSB of the red channel. ~1 is a bitwise NOT operation that creates a mask with all bits set except the LSB.
            - | data_bits[data_index]: Sets the LSB of the red channel to the current bit from data_bits. The | operator performs a bitwise OR operation.
        - data_index += 1: Advances the index to the next bit in data_bits.
        - new_pixels.append((r, g, b)): Appends the modified pixel to the new_pixels list.
    - else:: If all bits have been embedded, simply append the original pixel to new_pixels.

Save the Modified Image

```
img.putdata(new_pixels)
img.save(output_image_path)
print(f"Data embedded in {output_image_path}")
```

- Purpose: Updates the image with the modified pixels and saves it to the specified output path.
- Detail:
    - img.putdata(new_pixels): Replaces the image's pixel data with the new_pixels list.

- img.save(output_image_path): Saves the modified image to the file specified by output_image_path. This image now contains the hidden data.
- print(f"Data embedded in {output_image_path}"): Prints a confirmation message indicating that the data has been successfully embedded in the image.

Summary

The embed_data_in_image() function performs the following steps to embed data into an image using LSB steganography:

1. Opens the image and retrieves its pixel data.
2. Converts the data to hide into a list of bits.
3. Processes each pixel, modifying the least significant bit of the red channel to embed the data bits.
4. Saves the modified image with the hidden data.

This technique ensures that the hidden data does not noticeably affect the appearance of the image.

extract_data_from_image() Function

The extract_data_from_image() function is designed to retrieve hidden data from an image that was previously embedded using Least Significant Bit (LSB) steganography. Here's a detailed breakdown of how this function works:

Function Definition

```
def extract_data_from_image(image_path, data_size_in_bits):
```

- Purpose: Defines a function named extract_data_from_image that takes two parameters:
  - image_path: The file path of the image from which data needs to be extracted.
  - data_size_in_bits: The total number of bits that were embedded in the image. This helps determine how many bits to extract.

Open Image and Extract Pixels

```
img = Image.open(image_path)
pixels = list(img.getdata())
```

- Purpose: Opens the specified image and retrieves its pixel data.
- Detail:
    - Image.open(image_path): Opens the image file specified by image_path. The Image class from PIL (Python Imaging Library) is used for handling images.
    - img.getdata(): Retrieves the pixel data of the image. Each pixel is represented as a tuple (or a list) of RGB values (Red, Green, Blue).
    - list(img.getdata()): Converts the pixel data into a list of tuples. This makes it easier to process individual pixel values.

Initialize List for Data Bits

```
data_bits = []
```

- Purpose: Initializes an empty list named data_bits to store the extracted bits.

Extract Data Bits from Pixels

```
    for pixel in pixels[:data_size_in_bits]:  # Only extract the number of bits we know exist
        r, g, b = pixel[:3]
        data_bits.append(r & 1)  # Extract the LSB from the red channel
```

- Purpose: Iterates over a portion of the pixel data to extract the least significant bit (LSB) from the red channel of each pixel.
- Detail:
    - for pixel in pixels[:data_size_in_bits]:: Loops through the first data_size_in_bits pixels from the image. This ensures that only the number of pixels corresponding to the amount of embedded data are processed.
    - r, g, b = pixel[:3]: Extracts the red, green, and blue values from each pixel tuple. Only the red channel is used for extracting data.
    - data_bits.append(r & 1): Extracts the LSB from the red channel value:

- **r & 1**: Applies a bitwise AND operation between the red channel value and 1. This operation isolates the LSB, as 1 has all bits set to 0 except the least significant bit. The result is either 0 or 1, representing the extracted bit.

Convert Bits to Text

```
extracted_data = bits_to_text(data_bits)
```

- Purpose: Converts the list of extracted bits back into a readable text format.
- Detail:
    - bits_to_text(data_bits): Calls the bits_to_text function (described earlier) to convert the list of bits into a string of text.

Return the Extracted Data

```
return extracted_data
```

- Purpose: Returns the decoded text that was hidden in the image.

Summary

The extract_data_from_image() function performs the following steps to retrieve hidden data from an image:
1. Opens the image and retrieves its pixel data.
2. Extracts the least significant bits (LSBs) from the red channel of the specified number of pixels.
3. Converts the extracted bits into text using the bits_to_text function.
4. Returns the extracted text data.

This function is complementary to the embed_data_in_image function, which embeds data in the image using LSB steganography. The key idea is to reverse the process by extracting the same bits that were modified for embedding the data.

Output

```
DSA keys generated.
Data signed.
Data embedded in image_with_hidden_data.png
Extracted Data: Financial Transaction Report: Total= $5000
Extracted Signature:
HJCZhyV1QdVFhd5+OC35Pg5i2vPB9Vb48Nt6XsxvPpcYfiJwj8lTEm6hcyEUsalR/VnSCAipUCs=
Signature is valid.
```

Project 10: GUI Tkinter for Hiding Confidential Message with DSA and LSB Steganography

This project is a graphical user interface (GUI) application built with Python's Tkinter library, which focuses on Digital Signature Algorithm (DSA) encryption and steganography. The application allows users to generate DSA keys, sign and verify data, and embed or extract data from images using steganography techniques. The interface is designed to be user-friendly and integrates various functionalities through tabs, making it a comprehensive tool for cryptographic and data hiding tasks.

The core functionalities of the application include key generation, data signing, and data verification. Users can generate a pair of DSA keys, which are saved as PEM files. The private key is used to sign data, producing a cryptographic signature, while the public key is used to verify the authenticity of the signature. The application uses the Crypto library to handle cryptographic operations and provides text areas for displaying keys and signatures.

In addition to cryptographic functions, the application incorporates steganography features to hide data within images. Users can select an image, embed a message into it, and then save the modified image. The data is embedded by altering the least significant bit of the image's pixel values. The application also supports the extraction of hidden data from images, allowing users to retrieve and display the embedded information.

The GUI is structured into several tabs, each serving a different purpose. The Key Generation tab allows users to generate and display DSA keys. The Sign Data tab enables users to input a message, sign it using the generated private key, and view the signature. The Verify Data tab allows users to input a message and signature to verify its authenticity. The Image Embedding and Extraction tabs facilitate the embedding and extraction of data from images, respectively.

The application handles file operations, such as reading and writing keys, and supports basic error handling to guide users through the process. It includes feedback mechanisms, such as message boxes, to inform users about the status of their operations, such as successful key generation or errors in data entry. The use of Tkinter's Text and Entry widgets ensures that users can easily input and view large amounts of text data.

Overall, this project demonstrates a practical application of DSA encryption and steganography techniques, packaged into a user-friendly GUI. It integrates various cryptographic and data-hiding functionalities into a cohesive application, making it a valuable tool for users interested in exploring encryption and data security. The combination of these features in a single application showcases the versatility and power of Python for developing cryptographic and data manipulation tools.

```python
import tkinter as tk
from tkinter import filedialog, messagebox, ttk
from PIL import Image, ImageTk
from Crypto.PublicKey import DSA
from Crypto.Signature import DSS
from Crypto.Hash import SHA256
import base64
import os

# Helper functions
def text_to_bits(text):
    bits = []
    for char in text:
        bits.extend([int(bit) for bit in format(ord(char), '08b')])
    return bits

def bits_to_text(bits):
    chars = []
    for i in range(0, len(bits), 8):
        byte = bits[i:i + 8]
        byte_str = ''.join([str(bit) for bit in byte])
        chars.append(chr(int(byte_str, 2)))
    return ''.join(chars)

def generate_dsa_keys(private_key_path, public_key_path):
    key = DSA.generate(2048)
    private_key = key.export_key()
    public_key = key.publickey().export_key()

    with open(private_key_path, 'wb') as priv_file:
        priv_file.write(private_key)

    with open(public_key_path, 'wb') as pub_file:
        pub_file.write(public_key)

def sign_data(private_key_path, data):
    with open(private_key_path, 'rb') as key_file:
```

```python
        private_key = DSA.import_key(key_file.read())

    hash_obj = SHA256.new(data.encode())
    signer = DSS.new(private_key, 'fips-186-3')
    signature = signer.sign(hash_obj)

    signature_base64 = base64.b64encode(signature).decode()
    return signature_base64

def verify_data(public_key_path, data, signature_base64):
    with open(public_key_path, 'rb') as key_file:
        public_key = DSA.import_key(key_file.read())

    hash_obj = SHA256.new(data.encode())
    verifier = DSS.new(public_key, 'fips-186-3')

    signature = base64.b64decode(signature_base64)

    try:
        verifier.verify(hash_obj, signature)
        return True
    except ValueError:
        return False

def embed_data_in_image(image_path, output_image_path, data_to_hide):
    img = Image.open(image_path)
    pixels = list(img.getdata())

    data_bits = text_to_bits(data_to_hide)
    data_len = len(data_bits)
    data_index = 0

    new_pixels = []

    for pixel in pixels:
        if data_index < data_len:
            r, g, b = pixel[:3]
            r = (r & ~1) | data_bits[data_index]
            data_index += 1
            new_pixels.append((r, g, b))
        else:
            new_pixels.append(pixel)

    img.putdata(new_pixels)
    img.save(output_image_path)

def extract_data_from_image(image_path, data_size_in_bits):
    img = Image.open(image_path)
    pixels = list(img.getdata())

    data_bits = []

    for pixel in pixels[:data_size_in_bits]:
        r, g, b = pixel[:3]
        data_bits.append(r & 1)

    extracted_data = bits_to_text(data_bits)
    return extracted_data
```

```python
# GUI Application
class DSAApp:
    def __init__(self, root):
        self.root = root
        self.root.title("DSA Encryption & Steganography")
        self.root.geometry("1000x600")

        self.notebook = ttk.Notebook(root)
        self.notebook.pack(expand=True, fill='both')

        self.create_tabs()

    def create_tabs(self):
        # Key Generation Tab
        self.key_tab = ttk.Frame(self.notebook)
        self.notebook.add(self.key_tab, text='Key Generation')

        self.generate_keys_button = tk.Button(self.key_tab, text="Generate DSA Keys", command=self.generate_keys)
        self.generate_keys_button.pack(pady=20)

        # Private and Public Key Display
        self.private_key_text = tk.Text(self.key_tab, height=10, width=100)
        self.private_key_text.pack(pady=10)
        self.public_key_text = tk.Text(self.key_tab, height=10, width=100)
        self.public_key_text.pack(pady=10)

        # Signing Tab
        self.sign_tab = ttk.Frame(self.notebook)
        self.notebook.add(self.sign_tab, text='Sign Data')

        self.sign_message_entry = tk.Entry(self.sign_tab, width=50)
        self.sign_message_entry.pack(pady=10)

        self.sign_button = tk.Button(self.sign_tab, text="Sign Data", command=self.sign_data)
        self.sign_button.pack(pady=10)

        # Use Text widget for signature
        self.signature_text = tk.Text(self.sign_tab, height=10, width=100)
        self.signature_text.pack(pady=10)

        # Verification Tab
        self.verify_tab = ttk.Frame(self.notebook)
        self.notebook.add(self.verify_tab, text='Verify Data')

        self.verify_message_entry = tk.Entry(self.verify_tab, width=50)
        self.verify_message_entry.pack(pady=10)

        # Use Text widget for signature verification
        self.signature_verify_text = tk.Text(self.verify_tab, height=10, width=100)
        self.signature_verify_text.pack(pady=10)

        self.verify_button = tk.Button(self.verify_tab, text="Verify Data", command=self.verify_data)
        self.verify_button.pack(pady=10)
```

```python
        # Image Embedding Tab
        self.embed_tab = ttk.Frame(self.notebook)
        self.notebook.add(self.embed_tab, text='Embed Data in Image')

        self.select_image_button = tk.Button(self.embed_tab, text="Select Image", command=self.browse_image_to_embed)
        self.select_image_button.pack(pady=10)

        self.embed_message_entry = tk.Entry(self.embed_tab, width=50)
        self.embed_message_entry.pack(pady=10)

        self.embed_button = tk.Button(self.embed_tab, text="Embed Data", command=self.embed_data)
        self.embed_button.pack(pady=10)

        self.embed_image_label = tk.Label(self.embed_tab)
        self.embed_image_label.pack(pady=10)

        # Image Extraction Tab
        self.extract_tab = ttk.Frame(self.notebook)
        self.notebook.add(self.extract_tab, text='Extract Data from Image')

        self.select_extract_image_button = tk.Button(self.extract_tab, text="Select Image", command=self.browse_image_to_extract)
        self.select_extract_image_button.pack(pady=10)

        self.extract_button = tk.Button(self.extract_tab, text="Extract Data", command=self.extract_data)
        self.extract_button.pack(pady=10)

        self.extracted_data_text = tk.Text(self.extract_tab, height=10, width=80)
        self.extracted_data_text.pack(pady=10)

        self.extract_image_label = tk.Label(self.extract_tab)
        self.extract_image_label.pack(pady=10)

    def generate_keys(self):
        private_key_path = 'private_key.pem'
        public_key_path = 'public_key.pem'
        generate_dsa_keys(private_key_path, public_key_path)

        # Display keys in text areas
        with open(private_key_path, 'rb') as priv_file:
            private_key = priv_file.read().decode()
            self.private_key_text.delete(1.0, tk.END)
            self.private_key_text.insert(tk.END, private_key)

        with open(public_key_path, 'rb') as pub_file:
            public_key = pub_file.read().decode()
            self.public_key_text.delete(1.0, tk.END)
            self.public_key_text.insert(tk.END, public_key)

        messagebox.showinfo("Info", "DSA keys generated and displayed.")

    def sign_data(self):
        private_key_path = 'private_key.pem'
        message = self.sign_message_entry.get()
        if not message:
```

```python
            messagebox.showerror("Error", "Message cannot be empty.")
            return

        signature = sign_data(private_key_path, message)
        self.signature_text.delete(1.0, tk.END)
        self.signature_text.insert(tk.END, signature)
        messagebox.showinfo("Info", "Data signed.")

    def verify_data(self):
        public_key_path = 'public_key.pem'
        message = self.verify_message_entry.get()
        signature_base64 = self.signature_verify_text.get(1.0, tk.END).strip()
        if not message or not signature_base64:
            messagebox.showerror("Error", "Message and Signature cannot be empty.")
            return

        valid = verify_data(public_key_path, message, signature_base64)
        if valid:
            messagebox.showinfo("Info", "Signature is valid.")
        else:
            messagebox.showerror("Error", "Signature is invalid.")

    def browse_image_to_embed(self):
        self.image_to_embed = filedialog.askopenfilename(filetypes=[("Image Files", "*.png;*.jpg;*.jpeg")])
        if self.image_to_embed:
            self.display_image(self.embed_image_label, self.image_to_embed)
            messagebox.showinfo("Info", "Image selected for embedding data.")

    def embed_data(self):
        if not hasattr(self, 'image_to_embed'):
            messagebox.showerror("Error", "No image selected.")
            return

        data_to_hide = self.embed_message_entry.get()
        if not data_to_hide:
            messagebox.showerror("Error", "Data to hide cannot be empty.")
            return

        output_image_path = 'image_with_hidden_data.png'
        embed_data_in_image(self.image_to_embed, output_image_path, data_to_hide)
        messagebox.showinfo("Info", "Data embedded in image.")

    def browse_image_to_extract(self):
        self.image_to_extract = filedialog.askopenfilename(filetypes=[("Image Files", "*.png;*.jpg;*.jpeg")])
        if self.image_to_extract:
            self.display_image(self.extract_image_label, self.image_to_extract)
            messagebox.showinfo("Info", "Image selected for data extraction.")

    def extract_data(self):
        if not hasattr(self, 'image_to_extract'):
            messagebox.showerror("Error", "No image selected.")
            return

        data_size_in_bits = len(text_to_bits(self.embed_message_entry.get()))  # Assuming the same length
```

```
            extracted_data_with_signature = 
extract_data_from_image(self.image_to_extract, data_size_in_bits)

        if extracted_data_with_signature:
            parts = extracted_data_with_signature.rsplit("\nSignature: ", 1)
            if len(parts) == 2:
                extracted_data, extracted_signature = parts
                self.extracted_data_text.delete(1.0, tk.END)
                self.extracted_data_text.insert(tk.END, f"Extracted Data: 
{extracted_data}\nExtracted Signature: {extracted_signature}")
                messagebox.showinfo("Info", "Data extracted from image.")
            else:
                self.extracted_data_text.delete(1.0, tk.END)
                self.extracted_data_text.insert(tk.END, f"Extracted Data: 
{extracted_data_with_signature}")
                messagebox.showwarning("Warning", "Signature not found in extracted 
data.")
        else:
            messagebox.showerror("Error", "No data found in the image.")

    def display_image(self, label, image_path):
        image = Image.open(image_path)
        image = image.resize((300, 300), Image.LANCZOS)  # Use Image.LANCZOS for 
resampling
        photo = ImageTk.PhotoImage(image)
        label.config(image=photo)
        label.image = photo

# Main execution
if __name__ == "__main__":
    root = tk.Tk()
    app = DSAApp(root)
    root.mainloop()
```

Let's break down each part of the code:

Class Initialization

```
class DSAApp:
    def __init__(self, root):
        self.root = root
        self.root.title("DSA Encryption & Steganography")
        self.root.geometry("1000x600")
```

- class DSAApp: Defines a new class named DSAApp.
- def __init__(self, root): The initializer method for the class. It sets up the main window of the application.
- self.root = root: Stores the root window (the main application window) in an instance variable.

- self.root.title("DSA Encryption & Steganography"): Sets the title of the main window.
- self.root.geometry("1000x600"): Defines the initial size of the window (1000x600 pixels).

Notebook and Tabs Setup

```
self.notebook = ttk.Notebook(root)
self.notebook.pack(expand=True, fill='both')

self.create_tabs()
```

- self.notebook = ttk.Notebook(root): Creates a Notebook widget to handle tabbed interfaces.
- self.notebook.pack(expand=True, fill='both'): Packs the Notebook widget to expand and fill the main window.
- self.create_tabs(): Calls the method to set up different tabs within the Notebook.

Tab Creation

```
def create_tabs(self):
    # Key Generation Tab
    self.key_tab = ttk.Frame(self.notebook)
    self.notebook.add(self.key_tab, text='Key Generation')

    self.generate_keys_button = tk.Button(self.key_tab, text="Generate DSA Keys", command=self.generate_keys)
    self.generate_keys_button.pack(pady=20)

    # Private and Public Key Display
    self.private_key_text = tk.Text(self.key_tab, height=10, width=100)
    self.private_key_text.pack(pady=10)
    self.public_key_text = tk.Text(self.key_tab, height=10, width=100)
    self.public_key_text.pack(pady=10)
```

- self.key_tab = ttk.Frame(self.notebook): Creates a new tab frame for the Key Generation tab.
- self.notebook.add(self.key_tab, text='Key Generation'): Adds this frame as a tab to the Notebook with the label 'Key Generation'.
- self.generate_keys_button: A button to generate DSA keys, which triggers the generate_keys method.

- self.private_key_text and self.public_key_text: Text widgets to display the private and public keys, respectively.

Signing Tab

```
# Signing Tab
self.sign_tab = ttk.Frame(self.notebook)
self.notebook.add(self.sign_tab, text='Sign Data')

self.sign_message_entry = tk.Entry(self.sign_tab, width=50)
self.sign_message_entry.pack(pady=10)

self.sign_button = tk.Button(self.sign_tab, text="Sign Data", command=self.sign_data)
self.sign_button.pack(pady=10)

# Use Text widget for signature
self.signature_text = tk.Text(self.sign_tab, height=10, width=100)
self.signature_text.pack(pady=10)
```

- self.sign_tab = ttk.Frame(self.notebook): Creates a new tab frame for signing data.
- self.notebook.add(self.sign_tab, text='Sign Data'): Adds this frame as a tab to the Notebook with the label 'Sign Data'.
- self.sign_message_entry: Entry widget to input the message to be signed.
- self.sign_button: Button to sign the message, triggering the sign_data method.
- self.signature_text: Text widget to display the generated signature.

Verification Tab

```
# Verification Tab
self.verify_tab = ttk.Frame(self.notebook)
self.notebook.add(self.verify_tab, text='Verify Data')

self.verify_message_entry = tk.Entry(self.verify_tab, width=50)
self.verify_message_entry.pack(pady=10)

# Use Text widget for signature verification
self.signature_verify_text = tk.Text(self.verify_tab, height=10, width=100)
self.signature_verify_text.pack(pady=10)

self.verify_button = tk.Button(self.verify_tab, text="Verify Data", command=self.verify_data)
self.verify_button.pack(pady=10)
```

- self.verify_tab = ttk.Frame(self.notebook): Creates a new tab frame for verifying signatures.
- self.notebook.add(self.verify_tab, text='Verify Data'): Adds this frame as a tab to the Notebook with the label 'Verify Data'.
- self.verify_message_entry: Entry widget for the message to verify.
- self.signature_verify_text: Text widget to input the signature to be verified.
- self.verify_button: Button to verify the signature, triggering the verify_data method.

Image Embedding Tab

```
# Image Embedding Tab
self.embed_tab = ttk.Frame(self.notebook)
self.notebook.add(self.embed_tab, text='Embed Data in Image')

self.select_image_button = tk.Button(self.embed_tab, text="Select Image", 
command=self.browse_image_to_embed)
self.select_image_button.pack(pady=10)

self.embed_message_entry = tk.Entry(self.embed_tab, width=50)
self.embed_message_entry.pack(pady=10)

self.embed_button = tk.Button(self.embed_tab, text="Embed Data", 
command=self.embed_data)
self.embed_button.pack(pady=10)

self.embed_image_label = tk.Label(self.embed_tab)
self.embed_image_label.pack(pady=10)
```

- self.embed_tab = ttk.Frame(self.notebook): Creates a new tab frame for embedding data in an image.
- self.notebook.add(self.embed_tab, text='Embed Data in Image'): Adds this frame as a tab to the Notebook with the label 'Embed Data in Image'.
- self.select_image_button: Button to select an image file, triggering the browse_image_to_embed method.
- self.embed_message_entry: Entry widget for the message to embed in the image.
- self.embed_button: Button to embed the data into the selected image, triggering the embed_data method.
- self.embed_image_label: Label to display the selected image.

Image Extraction Tab

```
    # Image Extraction Tab
    self.extract_tab = ttk.Frame(self.notebook)
    self.notebook.add(self.extract_tab, text='Extract Data from Image')

    self.select_extract_image_button = tk.Button(self.extract_tab, text="Select
Image", command=self.browse_image_to_extract)
    self.select_extract_image_button.pack(pady=10)

    self.extract_button = tk.Button(self.extract_tab, text="Extract Data",
command=self.extract_data)
    self.extract_button.pack(pady=10)

    self.extracted_data_text = tk.Text(self.extract_tab, height=10, width=80)
    self.extracted_data_text.pack(pady=10)

    self.extract_image_label = tk.Label(self.extract_tab)
    self.extract_image_label.pack(pady=10)
```

- self.extract_tab = ttk.Frame(self.notebook): Creates a new tab frame for extracting data from an image.
- self.notebook.add(self.extract_tab, text='Extract Data from Image'): Adds this frame as a tab to the Notebook with the label 'Extract Data from Image'.
- self.select_extract_image_button: Button to select an image file for data extraction, triggering the browse_image_to_extract method.
- self.extract_button: Button to extract data from the selected image, triggering the extract_data method.
- self.extracted_data_text: Text widget to display the extracted data.
- self.extract_image_label: Label to display the selected image for extraction.

Key Generation

```
def generate_keys(self):
    private_key_path = 'private_key.pem'
    public_key_path = 'public_key.pem'
    generate_dsa_keys(private_key_path, public_key_path)

    # Display keys in text areas
    with open(private_key_path, 'rb') as priv_file:
        private_key = priv_file.read().decode()
        self.private_key_text.delete(1.0, tk.END)
        self.private_key_text.insert(tk.END, private_key)

    with open(public_key_path, 'rb') as pub_file:
        public_key = pub_file.read().decode()
        self.public_key_text.delete(1.0, tk.END)
```

```
        self.public_key_text.insert(tk.END, public_key)
    messagebox.showinfo("Info", "DSA keys generated and displayed.")
```

- generate_keys(self): Method to generate DSA keys.
- private_key_path and public_key_path: File paths for storing the generated keys.
- generate_dsa_keys(): Function call to generate DSA keys (assumed to be defined elsewhere).
- with open(...): Opens the key files, reads their contents, and displays them in the respective text widgets.
- messagebox.showinfo(...): Displays a message box indicating that keys have been generated and displayed.

Signing Data

```
def sign_data(self):
    private_key_path = 'private_key.pem'
    message = self.sign_message_entry.get()
    if not message:
        messagebox.showerror("Error", "Message cannot be empty.")
        return

    signature = sign_data(private_key_path, message)
    self.signature_text.delete(1.0, tk.END)
    self.signature_text.insert(tk.END, signature)
    messagebox.showinfo("Info", "Data signed.")
```

- sign_data(self): Method to sign data using the DSA private key.
- private_key_path: Path to the private key.
- message: Retrieves the message from the entry widget.
- if not message: Checks if the message is empty and shows an error message if true.
- signature = sign_data(...): Function call to sign the data (assumed to be defined elsewhere).
- self.signature_text.delete(1.0, tk.END): Clears the text widget before inserting the new signature.
- messagebox.showinfo(...): Displays a message box indicating that the data has been signed.

Verifying Data

```
def verify_data(self):
    public_key_path = 'public_key.pem'
    message = self.verify_message_entry.get()
    signature_base64 = self.signature_verify_text.get(1.0, tk.END).strip()
    if not message or not signature_base64:
        messagebox.showerror("Error", "Message and Signature cannot be empty.")
        return

    valid = verify_data(public_key_path, message, signature_base64)
    if valid:
        messagebox.showinfo("Info", "Signature is valid.")
    else:
        messagebox.showerror("Error", "Signature is invalid.")
```

- verify_data(self): Method to verify the signature of a message using the DSA public key.
- public_key_path: Path to the public key.
- message: Retrieves the message from the entry widget.
- signature_base64: Retrieves and strips the signature from the text widget.
- if not message or not signature_base64: Checks if either field is empty and shows an error message if true.
- valid = verify_data(...): Function call to verify the data (assumed to be defined elsewhere).
- messagebox.showinfo(...): Displays a message box indicating whether the signature is valid.
- messagebox.showerror(...): Displays an error message if the signature is invalid.

Image Embedding

```
def browse_image_to_embed(self):
    self.image_to_embed = filedialog.askopenfilename(filetypes=[("Image Files",
"*.png;*.jpg;*.jpeg")])
    if self.image_to_embed:
        self.display_image(self.embed_image_label, self.image_to_embed)
        messagebox.showinfo("Info", "Image selected for embedding data.")
```

- browse_image_to_embed(self): Method to select an image file for embedding data.
- self.image_to_embed: Stores the path of the selected image.
- filedialog.askopenfilename(...): Opens a file dialog to select an image file.

- self.display_image(...): Displays the selected image in the label.
- messagebox.showinfo(...): Shows a message box indicating that the image has been selected.

Embedding Data

```
def embed_data(self):
    if not hasattr(self, 'image_to_embed'):
        messagebox.showerror("Error", "No image selected.")
        return

    data_to_hide = self.embed_message_entry.get()
    if not data_to_hide:
        messagebox.showerror("Error", "Data to hide cannot be empty.")
        return

    output_image_path = 'image_with_hidden_data.png'
    embed_data_in_image(self.image_to_embed, output_image_path, data_to_hide)
    messagebox.showinfo("Info", "Data embedded in image.")
```

- embed_data(self): Method to embed data into an image.
- if not hasattr(self, 'image_to_embed'): Checks if an image has been selected and shows an error if not.
- data_to_hide: Retrieves the data to be embedded from the entry widget.
- if not data_to_hide: Checks if the data is empty and shows an error if true.
- embed_data_in_image(...): Function call to embed the data into the selected image (assumed to be defined elsewhere).
- messagebox.showinfo(...): Shows a message box indicating that the data has been embedded.

Image Extraction

```
def browse_image_to_extract(self):
    self.image_to_extract = filedialog.askopenfilename(filetypes=[("Image Files",
"*.png;*.jpg;*.jpeg")])
    if self.image_to_extract:
        self.display_image(self.extract_image_label, self.image_to_extract)
        messagebox.showinfo("Info", "Image selected for data extraction.")
```

- browse_image_to_extract(self): Method to select an image file for data extraction.
- self.image_to_extract: Stores the path of the selected image.
- filedialog.askopenfilename(...): Opens a file dialog to select an image file.

- self.display_image(...): Displays the selected image in the label.
- messagebox.showinfo(...): Shows a message box indicating that the image has been selected for extraction.

Extracting Data

```
def extract_data(self):
    if not hasattr(self, 'image_to_extract'):
        messagebox.showerror("Error", "No image selected.")
        return

    data_size_in_bits = len(text_to_bits(self.embed_message_entry.get()))  # Assuming the same length
    extracted_data_with_signature = extract_data_from_image(self.image_to_extract, data_size_in_bits)

    if extracted_data_with_signature:
        parts = extracted_data_with_signature.rsplit("\nSignature: ", 1)
        if len(parts) == 2:
            extracted_data, extracted_signature = parts
            self.extracted_data_text.delete(1.0, tk.END)
            self.extracted_data_text.insert(tk.END, f"Extracted Data: {extracted_data}\nExtracted Signature: {extracted_signature}")
            messagebox.showinfo("Info", "Data extracted from image.")
        else:
            self.extracted_data_text.delete(1.0, tk.END)
            self.extracted_data_text.insert(tk.END, f"Extracted Data: {extracted_data_with_signature}")
            messagebox.showwarning("Warning", "Signature not found in extracted data.")
    else:
        messagebox.showerror("Error", "No data found in the image.")
```

- extract_data(self): Method to extract data from an image.
- if not hasattr(self, 'image_to_extract'): Checks if an image has been selected and shows an error if not.
- data_size_in_bits: Calculates the size of the data to be extracted, assuming it matches the original size.
- extracted_data_with_signature = extract_data_from_image(...): Function call to extract the data from the image (assumed to be defined elsewhere).
- if extracted_data_with_signature: Checks if any data was extracted.
- parts = extracted_data_with_signature.rsplit("\nSignature: ", 1): Splits the extracted data to separate it from the signature.
- if len(parts) == 2: If both data and signature are present, displays them separately.
- else: If only the data is present, shows a warning that the signature was not found.

- messagebox.showerror(...): Displays an error message if no data was found.

Display Image Method

```
def display_image(self, label, image_path):
    image = Image.open(image_path)
    image = image.resize((300, 300), Image.LANCZOS)  # Use Image.LANCZOS for resampling
    photo = ImageTk.PhotoImage(image)
    label.config(image=photo)
    label.image = photo
```

- display_image(self, label, image_path): Method to display an image in a label.
- image = Image.open(image_path): Opens the image file.
- image = image.resize((300, 300), Image.LANCZOS): Resizes the image to 300x300 pixels using the LANCZOS filter for high-quality resampling.
- photo = ImageTk.PhotoImage(image): Converts the image to a format that can be displayed in a Tkinter widget.
- label.config(image=photo): Updates the label to display the new image.
- label.image = photo: Keeps a reference to the image to prevent it from being garbage collected.

This class sets up a Tkinter GUI for DSA (Digital Signature Algorithm) key generation, signing, verifying, and embedding/extracting data in/from images. It utilizes various Tkinter widgets like Button, Entry, Text, and Label, and integrates with functions for cryptographic operations and image handling.

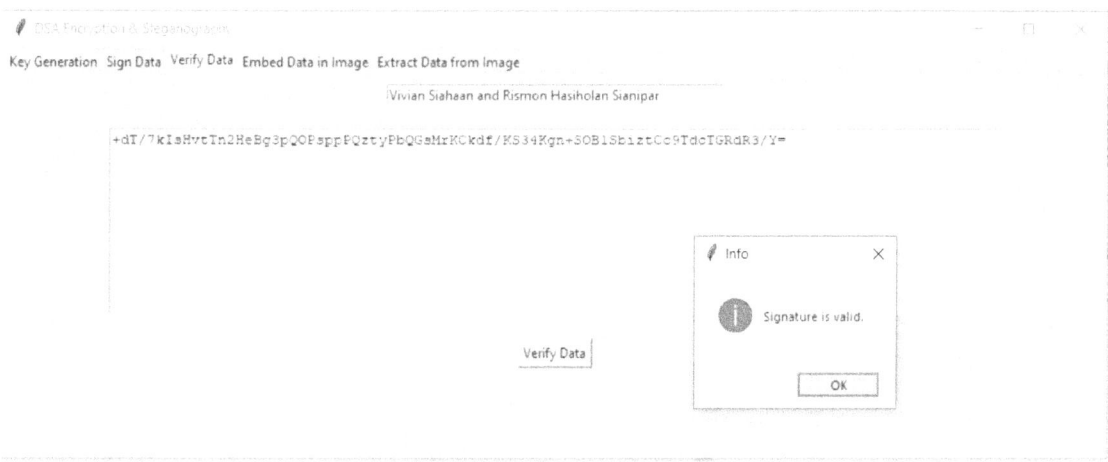

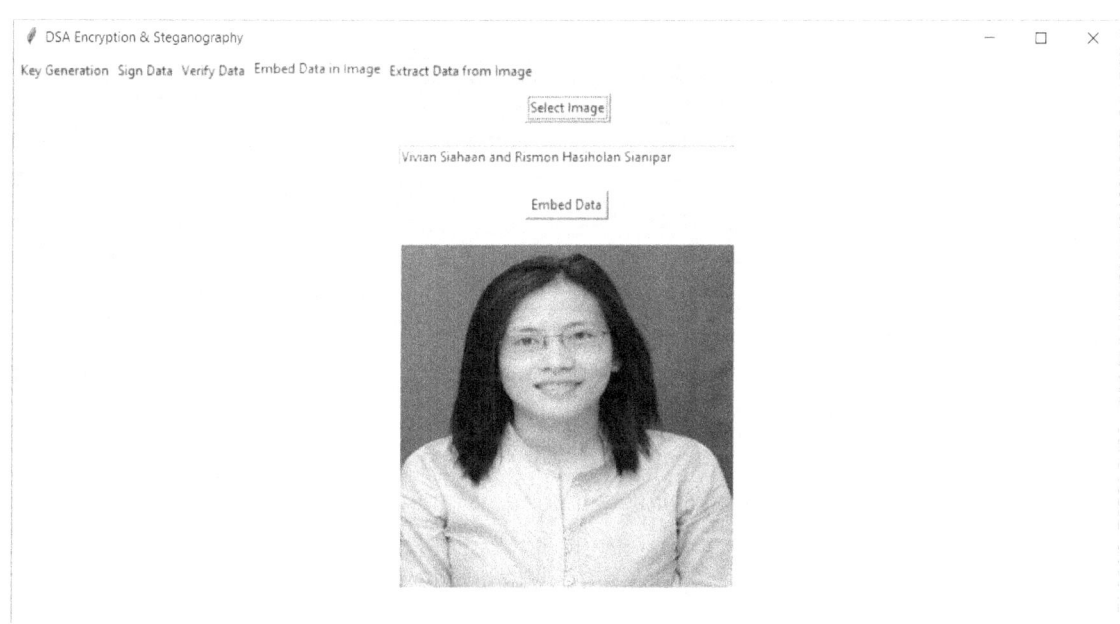

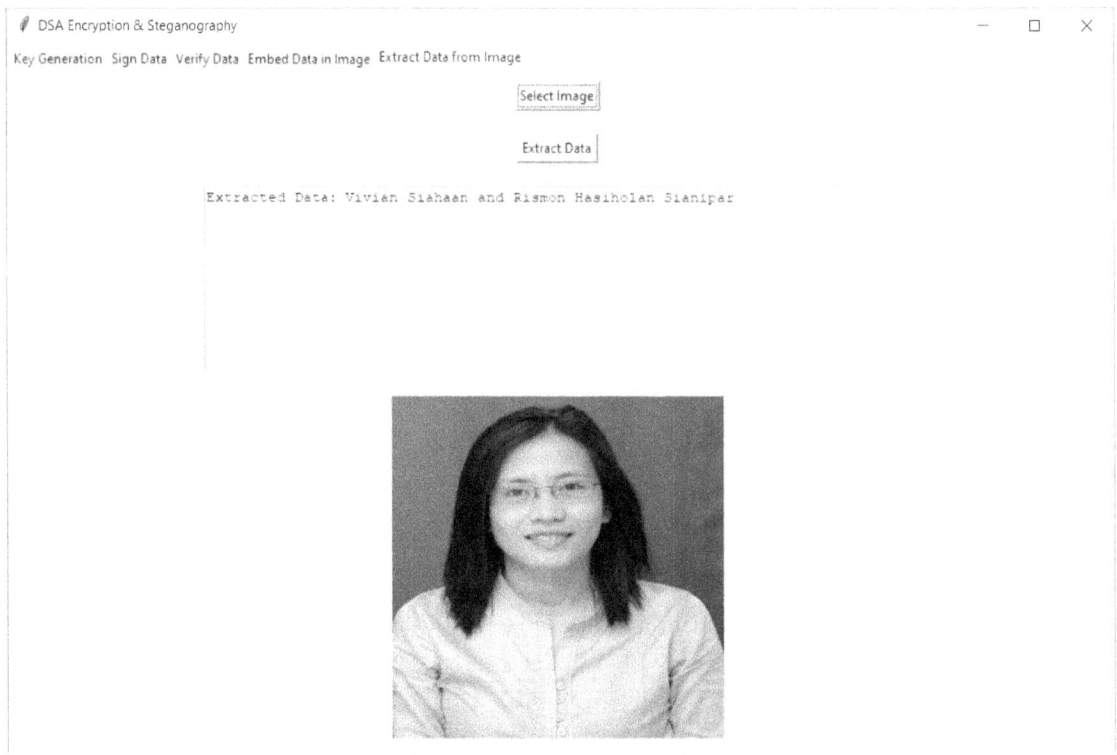

Project 11: Hiding Confidential Message with RSA and DSA Cryptographics Algorithm and LSB Steganography

This code demonstrates a complete workflow for encrypting and hiding data using RSA and DSA cryptographic algorithms and steganography. The workflow includes generating RSA and DSA keys, encrypting and signing data, embedding the encrypted and signed data into an image using LSB (Least Significant Bit) steganography, and then extracting and verifying the data. The process integrates multiple cryptographic techniques to ensure data confidentiality and integrity.

Initially, RSA keys are generated and saved to files. RSA encryption is used to encrypt a confidential message, and the encrypted data is then signed using a DSA private key. This dual-layer security ensures that the data is both confidential and authenticated. The encryption is performed with RSA's PKCS1_OAEP padding scheme, and the signature is created using DSA with the SHA-256 hash function, encoded in base64 for easy embedding.

The code then proceeds to embed the encrypted and signed data into an image. Using the Least Significant Bit (LSB) method of steganography, bits of the data are embedded into the image's pixel values, specifically altering the least significant bit of the red color channel. After embedding, the image is saved with the hidden data. For extraction, the hidden bits are read from the image, reconstructed into the original data format, and then separated into encrypted data and its signature.

Finally, the extracted data is verified and decrypted. The DSA signature is validated to confirm data integrity, and the RSA encrypted data is decrypted using the corresponding RSA private key. The decrypted message is then displayed. This process showcases a comprehensive method for securely transmitting data by combining encryption, digital signatures, and steganography, making it a robust solution for data protection in sensitive contexts.

```python
from PIL import Image
from Crypto.PublicKey import RSA, DSA
from Crypto.Signature import DSS
from Crypto.Hash import SHA256
from Crypto.Cipher import PKCS1_OAEP
import base64
import os

# Helper function to convert text to bits
def text_to_bits(text):
    bits = []
    for char in text:
        bits.extend([int(bit) for bit in format(ord(char), '08b')])
    return bits

# Helper function to convert bits to text
def bits_to_text(bits):
    chars = []
    for i in range(0, len(bits), 8):
        byte = bits[i:i + 8]
        byte_str = ''.join([str(bit) for bit in byte])
        chars.append(chr(int(byte_str, 2)))
    return ''.join(chars)

# Generate RSA keys and save them to files
def generate_rsa_keys(private_key_path, public_key_path):
    key = RSA.generate(2048)
    private_key = key.export_key()
    public_key = key.publickey().export_key()
```

```python
    with open(private_key_path, 'wb') as priv_file:
        priv_file.write(private_key)

    with open(public_key_path, 'wb') as pub_file:
        pub_file.write(public_key)

    print("RSA keys generated.")

# Encrypt data with RSA public key
def encrypt_data(public_key_path, data):
    with open(public_key_path, 'rb') as key_file:
        public_key = RSA.import_key(key_file.read())

    cipher = PKCS1_OAEP.new(public_key)
    encrypted_data = cipher.encrypt(data.encode())

    # Encode encrypted data as base64 for embedding
    encrypted_data_base64 = base64.b64encode(encrypted_data).decode()
    print("Data encrypted.")
    return encrypted_data_base64

# Decrypt data with RSA private key
def decrypt_data(private_key_path, encrypted_data_base64):
    with open(private_key_path, 'rb') as key_file:
        private_key = RSA.import_key(key_file.read())

    cipher = PKCS1_OAEP.new(private_key)
    encrypted_data = base64.b64decode(encrypted_data_base64)
    decrypted_data = cipher.decrypt(encrypted_data).decode()

    print("Data decrypted.")
    return decrypted_data

# Generate DSA keys and save them to files
def generate_dsa_keys(private_key_path, public_key_path):
    key = DSA.generate(2048)
    private_key = key.export_key()
    public_key = key.publickey().export_key()

    with open(private_key_path, 'wb') as priv_file:
        priv_file.write(private_key)

    with open(public_key_path, 'wb') as pub_file:
        pub_file.write(public_key)

    print("DSA keys generated.")

# Sign data with the private DSA key
```

```python
def sign_data(private_key_path, data):
    with open(private_key_path, 'rb') as key_file:
        private_key = DSA.import_key(key_file.read())

    hash_obj = SHA256.new(data.encode())
    signer = DSS.new(private_key, 'fips-186-3')
    signature = signer.sign(hash_obj)

    # Encode signature as base64 for embedding
    signature_base64 = base64.b64encode(signature).decode()
    print("Data signed.")
    return signature_base64

# Verify the data with the public DSA key
def verify_data(public_key_path, data, signature_base64):
    with open(public_key_path, 'rb') as key_file:
        public_key = DSA.import_key(key_file.read())

    hash_obj = SHA256.new(data.encode())
    verifier = DSS.new(public_key, 'fips-186-3')

    signature = base64.b64decode(signature_base64)

    try:
        verifier.verify(hash_obj, signature)
        print("Signature is valid.")
    except ValueError:
        print("Signature is invalid.")

# Embed data in image using LSB steganography
def embed_data_in_image(image_path, output_image_path, data_to_hide):
    img = Image.open(image_path)
    pixels = list(img.getdata())

    data_bits = text_to_bits(data_to_hide)
    data_len = len(data_bits)
    data_index = 0

    new_pixels = []

    for pixel in pixels:
        if data_index < data_len:
            r, g, b = pixel[:3]
            r = (r & ~1) | data_bits[data_index]  # Change the least significant bit of red channel
            data_index += 1
            new_pixels.append((r, g, b))
        else:
```

```python
            new_pixels.append(pixel)

    img.putdata(new_pixels)
    img.save(output_image_path)
    print(f"Data embedded in {output_image_path}")

# Extract data from image using LSB steganography
def extract_data_from_image(image_path, data_size_in_bits):
    img = Image.open(image_path)
    pixels = list(img.getdata())

    data_bits = []

    for pixel in pixels[:data_size_in_bits]:  # Only extract the number of bits we know exist
        r, g, b = pixel[:3]
        data_bits.append(r & 1)  # Extract the LSB from red channel

    extracted_data = bits_to_text(data_bits)
    return extracted_data

# Main function to demonstrate the process
def main():
    # Key paths
    rsa_private_key_path = 'rsa_private_key.pem'
    rsa_public_key_path = 'rsa_public_key.pem'
    dsa_private_key_path = 'dsa_private_key.pem'
    dsa_public_key_path = 'dsa_public_key.pem'

    # Step 1: Generate RSA and DSA keys
    generate_rsa_keys(rsa_private_key_path, rsa_public_key_path)
    generate_dsa_keys(dsa_private_key_path, dsa_public_key_path)

    # Step 2: Message to hide and sign
    confidential_message = "Financial Transaction Report: Total= $5000"

    # Step 3: Encrypt the message
    encrypted_data = encrypt_data(rsa_public_key_path, confidential_message)

    # Step 4: Sign the encrypted data
    signed_data = sign_data(dsa_private_key_path, encrypted_data)

    # Prepare data with signature for embedding
    data_to_hide = encrypted_data + "\nSignature: " + signed_data

    # Step 5: Embed signed data into image
```

```
    embed_data_in_image("input_image.png",
"image_with_hidden_data.png", data_to_hide)

    # Step 6: Extract the hidden data from the image
    extracted_data_with_signature =
extract_data_from_image("image_with_hidden_data.png",
len(text_to_bits(data_to_hide)))

    # Separate the extracted data from the signature
    extracted_data, extracted_signature =
extracted_data_with_signature.rsplit("\nSignature: ", 1)

    print(f"Extracted Encrypted Data: {extracted_data}")
    print(f"Extracted Signature: {extracted_signature}")

    # Step 7: Verify the extracted data
    verify_data(dsa_public_key_path, extracted_data,
extracted_signature)

    # Step 8: Decrypt the extracted data
    decrypted_data = decrypt_data(rsa_private_key_path, extracted_data)

    print(f"Decrypted Data: {decrypted_data}")

if __name__ == "__main__":
    main()
```

generate_rsa_keys() Function

The generate_rsa_keys() function is responsible for generating RSA key pairs and saving them to files. This process is crucial for public-key cryptography, where RSA (Rivest-Shamir-Adleman) is a widely used algorithm for secure data transmission. Here's a detailed breakdown of the function's operation:

RSA Key Generation:

```
key = RSA.generate(2048)
```

- This line creates a new RSA key pair using the RSA.generate method from the Crypto.PublicKey module. The argument 2048 specifies the key size in bits. A key size of 2048 bits is considered secure and is commonly used in practice. The key generation process involves the creation of both a public key and a private key.

These keys are mathematically linked; data encrypted with one key can only be decrypted with the other.

Exporting the Private Key:

```
private_key = key.export_key()
```

- After generating the RSA key pair, the private key is extracted using the export_key method. This method returns the private key in a format suitable for storage, typically PEM (Privacy-Enhanced Mail) format, which is a Base64-encoded representation of the key. The private key is essential for decrypting data that was encrypted with the corresponding public key and for signing data to verify authenticity.

Exporting the Public Key:

```
public_key = key.publickey().export_key()
```

- Similarly, the publickey method is used to retrieve the public key from the RSA key pair. The export_key method is then called on this public key object to obtain its PEM-encoded representation. The public key is used to encrypt data or verify signatures created with the corresponding private key. It can be shared openly without compromising security.

Saving the Keys to Files:

```
with open(private_key_path, 'wb') as priv_file:
    priv_file.write(private_key)

with open(public_key_path, 'wb') as pub_file:
    pub_file.write(public_key)
```

- The with open context manager is used to open files in binary write mode ('wb'). The private_key_path and public_key_path parameters specify the file paths where the keys will be saved. The write method is used to write the PEM-encoded key data to these files. By using binary mode, the function ensures that the key data is written exactly as it is without any encoding alterations.

Completion Message:

```
print("RSA keys generated.")
```

- Finally, the function prints a confirmation message indicating that the RSA keys have been successfully generated and saved. This is a simple way to notify the user or developer that the key generation process has been completed.

In summary, this function creates a pair of RSA keys (both public and private), exports them in a standard format, and saves them to specified files. This process is essential for setting up RSA-based encryption and decryption, and for performing operations such as digital signatures in secure communication systems.

encrypt_data() Function

The encrypt_data() function is used to encrypt data using an RSA public key. This function ensures that sensitive information is securely encrypted before it is shared or stored. Here's a detailed breakdown of the function's operation:

Reading the Public Key:

```
with open(public_key_path, 'rb') as key_file:
    public_key = RSA.import_key(key_file.read())
```

- The function begins by opening the file specified by public_key_path in binary read mode ('rb'). The file contains the RSA public key that will be used for encryption. The RSA.import_key method from the Crypto.PublicKey module reads the key data from the file and imports it into an RSA key object. This key object represents the public key and will be used to perform the encryption.

Setting Up the Encryption Cipher:

```
cipher = PKCS1_OAEP.new(public_key)
```

- The PKCS1_OAEP module is used to create an encryption cipher object with the imported public key. PKCS1_OAEP (Optimal Asymmetric Encryption Padding) is a padding scheme that enhances RSA encryption by adding padding to the plaintext before encryption. This padding helps protect against certain types of attacks and ensures that the encryption process is secure and robust.

Encrypting the Data:

```
encrypted_data = cipher.encrypt(data.encode())
```

- The encrypt method of the PKCS1_OAEP cipher object is called to encrypt the input data. The data.encode() method converts the data from a string to bytes, as encryption algorithms typically operate on byte data. The encrypt method processes the byte data with the RSA public key and returns the encrypted data in its raw, byte format.

Encoding Encrypted Data as Base64:

```
encrypted_data_base64 = base64.b64encode(encrypted_data).decode()
```

- Since the encrypted data is in a binary format, it is encoded into a Base64 string using base64.b64encode. Base64 encoding transforms binary data into an ASCII string format, making it easier to handle and embed in text-based formats (e.g., when storing in files or transmitting over text-based protocols). The decode() method converts the Base64 byte string into a regular string format.

Completion Message and Return:

```
print("Data encrypted.")
return encrypted_data_base64
```

- The function prints a confirmation message indicating that the data encryption process has been completed. It then returns the Base64-encoded encrypted data. This encoded string can be safely transmitted or stored, and it can later be decoded and decrypted using the corresponding RSA private key.

In summary, this function reads an RSA public key from a file, uses it to encrypt input data with PKCS1_OAEP padding, and then encodes the encrypted data in Base64 for easier handling. This process ensures that the data remains confidential and secure while being transferred or stored.

decrypt_data() Function

The decrypt_data() function is designed to decrypt data that has been previously encrypted using RSA encryption. This function is essential for securely recovering the original information from its encrypted form. Here's a detailed explanation of how it works:

Reading the Private Key:

```
with open(private_key_path, 'rb') as key_file:
    private_key = RSA.import_key(key_file.read())
```

- The function starts by opening the file specified by private_key_path in binary read mode ('rb'). This file contains the RSA private key used for decryption. The RSA.import_key method from the Crypto.PublicKey module is then used to read the key data from the file and import it into an RSA key object. This key object represents the private key necessary for decrypting the data.

Setting Up the Decryption Cipher:

```
cipher = PKCS1_OAEP.new(private_key)
```

- Similar to encryption, a PKCS1_OAEP cipher object is created, but this time with the imported RSA private key. The PKCS1_OAEP padding scheme used during encryption is also used here to ensure that the decryption process correctly reverses the padding applied during encryption.

Decoding Encrypted Data from Base64:

encrypted_data = base64.b64decode(encrypted_data_base64)

- The encrypted data is provided as a Base64-encoded string, so it must be converted back to its original binary format before decryption. The base64.b64decode function decodes the Base64 string, transforming it from an ASCII string representation back into its binary format. This step is necessary because the encrypted data was originally encoded in Base64 to make it suitable for text-based transmission and storage.

Decrypting the Data:

decrypted_data = cipher.decrypt(encrypted_data).decode()

- The decrypt method of the PKCS1_OAEP cipher object is then used to decrypt the binary data. This method reverses the RSA encryption and the PKCS1_OAEP padding applied earlier. The result is the original binary data, which is then decoded to a string format using .decode(). This converts the binary data back into a readable string format.

Completion Message and Return:

```
print("Data decrypted.")
return decrypted_data
```

- After successfully decrypting the data, the function prints a confirmation message indicating that the decryption process is complete. It then returns the decrypted data, which is now in its original, unencrypted form and can be used as needed.

In summary, this function reads the RSA private key from a file, uses it to decrypt Base64-encoded encrypted data with the PKCS1_OAEP padding scheme, and then decodes the resulting binary data into a readable string. This process ensures that the encrypted information can be securely and accurately recovered.

Output

```
RSA keys generated.
DSA keys generated.
Data encrypted.
Data signed.
Data embedded in image_with_hidden_data.png
Extracted Encrypted Data:
Fy/qBe0sQHiPI7sMs6Pn0itRGmA+EYjH5D/5jjRmEYgG4LVuedtTPBDWm29CeNgXIg8/PY0te6oKHpfM/k5M2
EVROI4BvjY9lgnW9ibZIja2Vi2YXCL+fR/g/+J5D8yDylmJxKz2SSWJTBVuTFU7jPYiRPsWRIDREBTX2w6101
iPyXUJ4v08k7lnm5WCgFVf/uZaRHxUjsWD3jGmO/PF0JB3j4kY1S0+sKVMooM5041OPwdWBUTtmLJHCBF6ugf
jJC/yQIvJdyNNWHl+98Cjyu1xip4ms6FCtwkOByQlw/m2taP39h2TOGLpPKQE8jHh0T9Iu7IQtY9EZVt6eUAk
GA==
Extracted Signature:
WowqUvDb4fsteZmQiY9cwpJ+Hb1+qILb2bYfJIHKpDzpis/vkxOBBJaGbmlgM+hxjCVs6PSAWFs=
Signature is valid.
Data decrypted.
Decrypted Data: Financial Transaction Report: Total= $5000
```

Project 12: GUI Tkinter for Hiding Confidential Message with RSA and DSA Cryptographics Algorithm and LSB Steganography

This project is a comprehensive cryptography tool implemented using the Tkinter library in Python. The application provides a graphical user interface (GUI) for key generation, data encryption and decryption, and steganography, making cryptographic operations accessible to users without needing command-line tools or complex programming knowledge. By integrating various cryptographic methods, this tool serves as an educational resource and a practical application for securely handling data.

The GUI is structured with a tabbed interface, separating functionality into three main sections: Key Generation, Encryption & Decryption, and Steganography. This structure allows users to navigate between different cryptographic operations easily. Each tab offers specific features with clear labels and buttons for generating keys, encrypting/decrypting data, and embedding/extracting hidden data in images. The use of scrolled text widgets for input and output makes the application user-friendly, providing ample space for displaying information and results.

In the Key Generation tab, the tool allows users to generate RSA and DSA keys. RSA (Rivest-Shamir-Adleman) and DSA (Digital Signature Algorithm) are widely used public-key cryptographic algorithms. RSA keys are generated with a length of 2048 bits, providing a good balance between security and performance. Users can save the generated keys to files, which can then be used for encryption, decryption, or digital signatures. The application informs the user upon successful key generation, ensuring transparency and user feedback.

The Encryption & Decryption tab allows users to perform asymmetric encryption and decryption using the RSA algorithm. Users can input plaintext data, which is then encrypted using the public key previously generated. The encryption process involves converting the plaintext into ciphertext, which is displayed in a base64-encoded format for ease of storage and transmission. For decryption, the user provides the base64-encoded ciphertext, which is then decrypted back to the original plaintext using the RSA private key. This demonstrates the secure transmission and retrieval of sensitive information.

The Steganography tab offers a unique functionality where users can embed data within an image. Steganography is the practice of hiding information within other, seemingly innocuous media. In this tool, users can select an image and input the data they wish to hide. The data is then converted into binary bits and embedded into the least significant bits of the image's pixels. This process modifies the image subtly, making it nearly impossible to detect the hidden data visually. The application also provides the capability to extract the hidden data from an image, demonstrating the complete cycle of data hiding and retrieval.

Overall, this project serves as a practical demonstration of cryptographic and steganographic techniques. It provides a user-friendly interface for generating cryptographic keys, encrypting and decrypting data, and embedding hidden messages in images. The use of RSA and DSA for key generation and encryption ensures secure data handling, while the steganography feature offers an additional layer of data concealment. This tool can be used for educational purposes, secure communication, or simply exploring the concepts of cryptography and data hiding in a hands-on manner.

```
import tkinter as tk
from tkinter import filedialog, messagebox, ttk
from tkinter import filedialog, messagebox, scrolledtext
from PIL import Image
from Crypto.PublicKey import RSA, DSA
from Crypto.Signature import DSS
from Crypto.Hash import SHA256
from Crypto.Cipher import PKCS1_OAEP
import base64
import os

class CryptoApp:
    def __init__(self, root):
        self.root = root
```

```python
        self.root.title("Cryptography Tool")
        self.create_widgets()

    def create_widgets(self):
        # Tabs
        self.tab_control = tk.ttk.Notebook(self.root)

        self.key_gen_tab = tk.Frame(self.tab_control)
        self.tab_control.add(self.key_gen_tab, text="Key Generation")
        self.create_key_gen_tab()

        self.encryption_tab = tk.Frame(self.tab_control)
        self.tab_control.add(self.encryption_tab, text="Encryption & Decryption")
        self.create_encryption_tab()

        self.steganography_tab = tk.Frame(self.tab_control)
        self.tab_control.add(self.steganography_tab, text="Steganography")
        self.create_steganography_tab()

        self.tab_control.pack(expand=1, fill="both")

    def create_key_gen_tab(self):
        # RSA Key Generation
        tk.Label(self.key_gen_tab, text="RSA Key Generation").pack(pady=5)
        tk.Button(self.key_gen_tab, text="Generate RSA Keys",
command=self.generate_rsa_keys).pack(pady=5)

        # DSA Key Generation
        tk.Label(self.key_gen_tab, text="DSA Key Generation").pack(pady=5)
        tk.Button(self.key_gen_tab, text="Generate DSA Keys",
command=self.generate_dsa_keys).pack(pady=5)

    def create_encryption_tab(self):
        # Encryption
        tk.Label(self.encryption_tab, text="Encrypt Data").pack(pady=5)
        self.encryption_input = tk.Text(self.encryption_tab, height=5, width=50)
        self.encryption_input.pack(pady=5)

        tk.Button(self.encryption_tab, text="Encrypt",
command=self.encrypt_data).pack(pady=5)
        self.encryption_output = scrolledtext.ScrolledText(self.encryption_tab,
height=5, width=50)
        self.encryption_output.pack(pady=5)

        # Decryption
        tk.Label(self.encryption_tab, text="Decrypt Data").pack(pady=5)
        self.decryption_input = tk.Text(self.encryption_tab, height=5, width=50)
        self.decryption_input.pack(pady=5)

        tk.Button(self.encryption_tab, text="Decrypt",
command=self.decrypt_data).pack(pady=5)
        self.decryption_output = scrolledtext.ScrolledText(self.encryption_tab,
height=5, width=50)
        self.decryption_output.pack(pady=5)

    def create_steganography_tab(self):
        # Steganography
        tk.Label(self.steganography_tab, text="Embed Data in Image").pack(pady=5)
```

```python
        tk.Button(self.steganography_tab, text="Select Image", 
command=self.select_image_to_embed).pack(pady=5)

        tk.Label(self.steganography_tab, text="Data to Hide").pack(pady=5)
        self.steganography_input = tk.Text(self.steganography_tab, height=5, 
width=50)
        self.steganography_input.pack(pady=5)

        tk.Button(self.steganography_tab, text="Embed Data", 
command=self.embed_data).pack(pady=5)

        tk.Label(self.steganography_tab, text="Extract Data from Image").pack(pady=5)
        tk.Button(self.steganography_tab, text="Select Image", 
command=self.select_image_to_extract).pack(pady=5)

        self.steganography_output = scrolledtext.ScrolledText(self.steganography_tab, 
height=5, width=50)
        self.steganography_output.pack(pady=5)

    def generate_rsa_keys(self):
        private_key_path = 'rsa_private_key.pem'
        public_key_path = 'rsa_public_key.pem'
        key = RSA.generate(2048)
        with open(private_key_path, 'wb') as priv_file:
            priv_file.write(key.export_key())
        with open(public_key_path, 'wb') as pub_file:
            pub_file.write(key.publickey().export_key())
        messagebox.showinfo("Info", "RSA keys generated and saved.")

    def generate_dsa_keys(self):
        private_key_path = 'dsa_private_key.pem'
        public_key_path = 'dsa_public_key.pem'
        key = DSA.generate(2048)
        with open(private_key_path, 'wb') as priv_file:
            priv_file.write(key.export_key())
        with open(public_key_path, 'wb') as pub_file:
            pub_file.write(key.publickey().export_key())
        messagebox.showinfo("Info", "DSA keys generated and saved.")

    def encrypt_data(self):
        public_key_path = 'rsa_public_key.pem'
        data = self.encryption_input.get("1.0", tk.END).strip()
        if not data:
            messagebox.showwarning("Warning", "No data to encrypt.")
            return

        with open(public_key_path, 'rb') as key_file:
            public_key = RSA.import_key(key_file.read())

        cipher = PKCS1_OAEP.new(public_key)
        encrypted_data = cipher.encrypt(data.encode())
        encrypted_data_base64 = base64.b64encode(encrypted_data).decode()
        self.encryption_output.delete("1.0", tk.END)
        self.encryption_output.insert(tk.END, encrypted_data_base64)

    def decrypt_data(self):
        private_key_path = 'rsa_private_key.pem'
        encrypted_data_base64 = self.decryption_input.get("1.0", tk.END).strip()
```

```python
            if not encrypted_data_base64:
                messagebox.showwarning("Warning", "No data to decrypt.")
                return

            with open(private_key_path, 'rb') as key_file:
                private_key = RSA.import_key(key_file.read())

            cipher = PKCS1_OAEP.new(private_key)
            encrypted_data = base64.b64decode(encrypted_data_base64)
            decrypted_data = cipher.decrypt(encrypted_data).decode()
            self.decryption_output.delete("1.0", tk.END)
            self.decryption_output.insert(tk.END, decrypted_data)

    def select_image_to_embed(self):
        self.image_path = filedialog.askopenfilename(filetypes=[("Image Files", 
"*.png;*.jpg;*.jpeg")])
        if not self.image_path:
            messagebox.showwarning("Warning", "No image selected.")

    def select_image_to_extract(self):
        self.image_path = filedialog.askopenfilename(filetypes=[("Image Files", 
"*.png;*.jpg;*.jpeg")])
        if not self.image_path:
            messagebox.showwarning("Warning", "No image selected.")
        else:
            # Extract data from image
            data_size = len(text_to_bits(self.steganography_input.get("1.0", 
tk.END).strip()))
            extracted_data = extract_data_from_image(self.image_path, data_size)
            self.steganography_output.delete("1.0", tk.END)
            self.steganography_output.insert(tk.END, extracted_data)

    def embed_data(self):
        data_to_hide = self.steganography_input.get("1.0", tk.END).strip()
        if not hasattr(self, 'image_path') or not self.image_path:
            messagebox.showwarning("Warning", "No image selected.")
            return
        if not data_to_hide:
            messagebox.showwarning("Warning", "No data to embed.")
            return

        output_image_path = "image_with_hidden_data.png"
        embed_data_in_image(self.image_path, output_image_path, data_to_hide)
        messagebox.showinfo("Info", f"Data embedded in {output_image_path}")

def text_to_bits(text):
    bits = []
    for char in text:
        bits.extend([int(bit) for bit in format(ord(char), '08b')])
    return bits

def bits_to_text(bits):
    chars = []
    for i in range(0, len(bits), 8):
        byte = bits[i:i + 8]
        byte_str = ''.join([str(bit) for bit in byte])
        chars.append(chr(int(byte_str, 2)))
    return ''.join(chars)
```

```python
def embed_data_in_image(image_path, output_image_path, data_to_hide):
    img = Image.open(image_path)
    pixels = list(img.getdata())
    data_bits = text_to_bits(data_to_hide)
    data_len = len(data_bits)
    data_index = 0
    new_pixels = []

    for pixel in pixels:
        if data_index < data_len:
            r, g, b = pixel[:3]
            r = (r & ~1) | data_bits[data_index]
            data_index += 1
            new_pixels.append((r, g, b))
        else:
            new_pixels.append(pixel)

    img.putdata(new_pixels)
    img.save(output_image_path)
    print(f"Data embedded in {output_image_path}")

def extract_data_from_image(image_path, data_size_in_bits):
    img = Image.open(image_path)
    pixels = list(img.getdata())
    data_bits = []

    for pixel in pixels[:data_size_in_bits]:
        r, g, b = pixel[:3]
        data_bits.append(r & 1)

    extracted_data = bits_to_text(data_bits)
    return extracted_data

if __name__ == "__main__":
    root = tk.Tk()
    app = CryptoApp(root)
    root.mainloop()
```

Cryptography Tool

Key Generation   Encryption & Decryption   Steganography

Embed Data in Image

[Select Image]

Data to Hide

```
Rismon Hasiholan Sianipar
```

[Embed Data]

Extract Data from Image

[Select Image]

```
Rismon Hasiholan Sianipar
```

www.ingramcontent.com/pod-product-compliance
Lightning Source LLC
Chambersburg PA
CBHW062106220526
45471CB00010B/3618